CORPORATE PLANNING IN PRACTICE

CORPORATE PLANNING IN PRACTICE

EDITED BY
John Fawn and Bernard Cox

Published in association with
The Strategic Planning Society
and
The Chartered Institute of Management Accountants

Kogan Page

First published in 1985 by the Institute of Cost
and Management Accountants

This edition first published in Great Britain in 1987 by
Kogan Page Ltd, 120 Pentonville Road, London N1 9JN,
by arrangement with the Chartered Institute of
Management Accountants.

British Library Cataloguing in Publication Data
Corporate planning in practice. — 2nd ed.
1. Corporate planning
I. Fawn, John II. Cox, Bernard, *1930–*
658.4'012 HD30.28

ISBN 1-85091-339-0

Printed and bound in Great Britain by
Mackays Ltd, Chatham, Kent.

Contents

List of illustrations

Acknowledgements

This book was prepared under the direction of a joint working party of the Institute of Cost and Management Accounting and The Strategic Planning Society. The working party, chaired by E.B. Bishop, FCMA JDipMA FCIS, Institute Medallist, included Christopher Ragg, Ray Kates and John Fawn. Russell Smallwood was secretary. Thanks are also due to Jackie Soloman of the ICMA Library, to the joint editors John Fawn and Bernard Cox and, of course, to the contributors who made the book possible.

The authors, editors and publishers are grateful to the Journal *Long Range Planning* for permission to reproduce Figure 1.1 on page 17; to Collier Macmillan for permission to reproduce Figure 1.4 on page 21, and to The *Harvard Business Review* for permission to reproduce the table on page 39.

About the contributors

David Allen FCMA JDipMA FCIS is a past President of the Institute of Cost and Management Accountants and serves on a number of institute committees. He has also published many journal articles and two books.

Following a commercial apprenticeship with the Owen Organisation he widened his experience of financial management in the UK and Europe, mostly with the Morgan Crucible Group. He joined the Cadbury Schweppes Group in 1972 and since 1979 has been on the Board of Cadbury Typhoo Ltd, where he heads the finance and logistics functions.

Bernard Cox MPhil FCMA FCCA started his career in management accountancy with a small company in heavy engineering. Further experience was gained with the Marconi Company and Westland Helicopters before taking up a senior appointment with a subsidiary of EMI.

Joining the staff of the Institute of Cost and Management Accountants in 1975, he now holds the post of Technical Director's Research, responsible for research and technical activities. He has published many journal articles and four books.

Basil Denning is a Vice-President and former Chairman of the Strategic Planning Society. He has wide experience as a company director, consultant and management educator specialising in business policy and strategy. Past appointments include a senior lectureship at the London Business School, Vice-President and Managing Partner, Harbridge House, London and Director of Standard Brands Ltd. He is currently a visiting fellow at the Management College, Henley, and maintains an independent consultancy practice.

John Fawn MA MSc graduated as an engineering scientist and has spent most of his career in the aero-engine business with Rolls-Royce. His early years as an engineer, designer and thermodynamicist were spent developing future-project aero engines. Later, he spent 8 years in the business and strategic planning areas.

He is now a lecturer in business policy at the Cranfield School of Management. He is also Director of the European Management of Technology Programme, a joint venture between Cranfield Institute of Technology (UK), the Technical University of Compiègne (France), the Technical University of Aachen (West Germany) and the Stockholm School of Economics (Sweden).

David Hussey BCom ACIS worked for the former Rhodesian Government in the field of economic planning and research. Returning to the UK after the dissolution of the Federation of Rhodesia and Nyasaland he formed a planning department in Union Carbide Ltd. He subsequently held appointments as the corporate manager in the Otis Elevator Co Ltd, Wander Ltd and the Fyffes Group.

Now Senior Vice-President and Managing Partner of Harbridge House, his work in consultancy has embraced the introduction of corporate planning, analysis of strategy and many other fields of study for clients from many sectors.

His books and articles have been widely published and he is a member of the Editorial Board of the SLRP journal 'Long Range Planning'.

William Hyde FCMA FCCA is a Past President of the Institute of Cost and Management Accountants and serves on a number of Institute Committees.

His early years in the Gas Industry involved him in many financial and administrative reorganisations and in the development of rolling corporate plans for his Board and the Industry.

In 1968 he was appointed industrial adviser to the merchant bank J. Henry Schroder Wagg & Co Ltd., becoming a director a year later. At this time he was involved in plans for diversification and development of client companies.

Following a period as a consultant he moved to the University of Oxford where he is now Secretary of the University Chest (Chief Financial Officer). This role includes responsibility for the University's investments as well as for financial matters generally.

Raymond Kates FCMA MInstM was group planning manager of Alfred Dunhill for six years until retiring early in 1983. He now combines lecturing at the Middlesex Business School and the Polytechnic of Central London with providing consultancy services in planning and finance. He has also published many articles.

During twelve years with Rockware Glass in the Finance and Marketing Divisions as Financial Planning Manager, he introduced planning into all the companies in the Group. He has also worked for AEC Ltd., Ford Motor Company and Rothmans International.

He is Director and past Vice-Chairman of the Strategic Planning Society, and represents this Society on the European Planning Federation. He is also a member of the Technical Activities Group of the ICMA.

Gerald Owen began his commercial career in 1962 with Dunlop Limited, where he spent twenty years in a number of appointments, starting as a research chemist at the group central research laboratories.

Dr. Owen subsequently held management posts in technical, manufacturing, planning and personnel functions as well as in general management, in the UK and overseas. For the period 1972-77 he was responsible for the Group's corporate planning function and was also secretary of the policy committee of the Dunlop/Pirrelli union.

Between 1974 and 1980 he was a non-executive director of Angus Fire Armour Ltd.

He joined the Burmah Group as Planning Director in 1982 and was appointed Director, Castrol marketing and technical development in April 1985.

John Pittaway graduated in mechanical sciences and economics from Cambridge University having also studied natural sciences at Oxford while in the Royal Navy.

He has worked as an engineer in the UK, Malaysia, Pakistan, Bangladesh and India. His first involvement with corporate planning was during his time in India where he was instrumental in designing and implementing a cybernetics-based works contracting system for Oil India Ltd in Upper Assam.

More recently he was General Manager, Operations and Planning for Burmah-Castrol and Chief Planning Officer – Technical in Burmah Oil Trading Ltd. Since 1983 he has been engaged in consultancy, providing advisory services to small businesses.

Foster Rogers trained as an engineer in the chemical process plant manufacturing industry before reading mathematics at the University of Keele. He then gained wide industrial experience as a Senior Functional Manager and Director of UK companies in the ceramic, textile and engineering industries.

As a Senior Lecturer at Derbyshire College he taught for several years the Corporate Planning Module on ICMA courses. He then accepted an invitation to become visiting Professor in the Institute of International Business at the Stockholm School of Economics. His current major research interest is concerned with global competition in high technology industries particularly in the aero-space industry.

Working with the Swedish Institute of Management he has developed training for international operations, a major international executive seminar for international managers.

Foster is widely travelled and conducts consultancy, courses and seminars in major industrial and academic centres in the UK, France, US, China and Middle East.

Introduction

John Fawn

In the early part of the industrial revolution running a business was a much less complicated process than today with fewer constraints than exist in the modern business world. Major projects, as large even as the building of the Great Western Railway, were planned as a totality and budgeted accordingly. The principles laid down by Adam Smith broadly held true. The year 1865 was a watershed as it was in that year that the first Companies Act passed through parliament and the concept of annual reporting was introduced.

Reporting profit and loss annually naturally leads to the need for a target or budget profit (or loss) for the coming year. Some business projects make sense only if longer time-scales are considered and may even then only be realistic as part of a total portfolio of projects. The options become so varied that there is rarely an optimum solution; the businessman's needs must live in an ill-defined environment.

Planning is an iterative process which is useful to the businessman as a method of coping with the uncertainties of the future. Business is a complicated process with many variables or decisions as inputs. Each decision tends to have an effect on other areas within the business matrix. Planning is a method of ensuring that decisions taken in different areas of a business are consistent and aimed at achieving a specific business goal.

The iterative process is best described in three stages:

1 trying to understand the environment, competitors in that environment, resources available and the style or culture of the business,
2 using the information gained to decide what future actions should be taken to further the business development,
3 implementing the decisions taken.

Any plan of action is worthless until action is taken. Successful action evolves from the coordination of a well-defined plan, the appropriate use of the formal organisation and information sources, knowledge and judicious use of the informal organisation systems that all companies have, and using the right people with the right skills.

Implementation closes the planning process iterative loop. The process of planning ensures that changes can be made since without change a company will be overtaken by the pressures of the competitive world. The successful implementation of plans puts a company in a stronger position within a dynamic environment, through its effect on the company culture, competitors, and resources. In this environment, further decisions have to be taken and implemented. Successful planning is a continuous process. Unsuccessful planning ensures that future changes will be resisted. It is important to a company that successful change occurs and therefore that the planning process is successful and accepted.

This book is designed to explore the process in simple stages. The authors have been invited to give their views of particular parts of the whole. Each chapter has its own style and brings the author's experiences to the attention of the reader. Some are immensely practical and others theoretical. This is a reflection of how different people approach life and its problems. Planning must indeed be flexible enough to take into account such variations.

There is some overlap, which provides the continuity for the book to flow properly and yet build on the expertise of the authors.

It is perhaps entirely logical that the Strategic Planning Society and the Institute of Cost and Management Accountants should collaborate to produce this publication. The former has a major interest and expertise in the strategic planning process. The latter provides professional guidance on the language of business and one of the major ways of presenting plans and translating those plans into actions.

The factors affecting planning

The first part of the book looks at the factors affecting a company and which should be taken into account when analysing options for the future.

The process cannot be done effectively on a random basis. Use of a check list is advocated for identifying important factors in the following order:

- the environment,
- the competition,
- resources available,
- the effect of culture and norms on the acceptability of given courses of action.

Analysis in this order can be directly compared with filtering. The first coarse filter identifies those factors which affect the whole community in the same way and on which little influence can be exerted. These major influences can be sifted out. The second identifies the way in which competition operates in a given sphere of influence or industry. Analysis of the resources available allows critical decisions on the acquisition and application of resources in the competitive battle. Finally an understanding of the culture and norms of a company will identify, within possible options, those courses of action which are most likely to be successful. The filters become finer as the analysis gets more complicated and planners can avoid effort on options that are unworkable.

Chapter 1 on the environment, by Basil Denning, explores the major elements that can affect any business. As a past chairman of the Strategic Planning Society he brings a great depth of knowledge to this area.

David Hussey, in Chapter 2, applies the second filter of analysis of competition. His consulting activities as director of Harbridge House allow him to bring a wide experience into his writing.

The next two chapters on resources available reflect two of the major constraints on businesses.

Bill Hyde, a past president of ICMA, presents in Chapter 3 an analysis of the problems of raising finance to complement retained earnings. These problems face practically all companies at some stage in their development. By contrast, Foster Rogers, a leading English academic based at one of Europe's leading business schools, takes a more theoretical look at long term capability planning. He considers in Chapter 4 the opportunities which can be created out of what has been traditionally regarded as an area which restricts opportunity in British business.

Chapter 5, by John Fawn, looks at the effect that company culture, style and individual people have on the success of a business. Even with the best planning and capability, a company is finally only as good as the people who direct and run the operation.

A complete analysis of these general factors puts a company in a position to make informed decisions on current and future strategy. It is up to the individual analyst to ensure that the factors he has chosen are appropriate and reflect the true position of a company. The factors suggested in this section are not exhaustive but merely give an impression of the processes that must be gone through. The analyst has a difficult job indeed.

Deciding company strategy

The completion of analysis brings companies to a stage of being able to make reasoned decisions. The actual process of decision taking is however very difficult. Chapters 6 and 7 deal with the process of how decisions are actually arrived at in companies.

There is a basic conflict in the process which must be resolved. At one extreme there is the need to involve everyone in the decision-making process in order to get the best possible inputs and greatest commitment to the decisions subsequently taken. At the other end of the spectrum is the need to see the problems from a detached point of view to get them in the right perspective. This is best done centrally at a senior level. The first is known as the bottom-up approach and the second as the top-down approach. Most companies take both approaches. The results of one are crosschecked against the other to ensure there are not too many discrepancies.

Chapter 6, by John Pittaway and Gerald Owen, describes how the process is enacted at a major British company which is respected for the way it handles its planning process.

Chapter 7, by John Fawn, describes some of the simple but effective top-down approaches developed by consulting companies and academics to enhance understanding. The pitfalls and difficulties of such methodology is also discussed.

During the 1980s there have been and will be developments in these techniques primarily associated with the capability of the computer to explore more and more scenarios. One of the keys to this lies in the computer's ability to digest options and calculate the implications almost instantaneously. Most important, however, is its ability to display the results in a simple, graphical and often colourful way that is easy to understand. You can ask politically unpalatable questions of a machine that, particularly in its modern microcomputer form, is able to provide answers in secret, and yet communicate vast quantities of relevant information into the company control system when required. Analysis is difficult but decision taking is crucial. Chapters 6 and 7 are intended as an insight into how to develop the skills of managing the decision-taking process.

The implementation of strategy

The creation of company strategy defines the tasks to be carried out. The best strategy cannot survive a poor implementation and yet a comparatively poor strategy can be successful if implemented well.

Implementation relies on two major factors:

- the formal organisation,
- the people involved and their informal communications structures.

The accounting structure is by far and away the most important formal organisation structure as it is the major information system within the company. Tasks cannot be performed without information on money, the only universal measure which can be found in all areas of a company. The accountancy system and the profession which supports it have a great responsibility therefore to ensure that the system realistically reflects what a company requires in order to be effective. David Allen's Chapter 8 looks at the integration of the accountancy system with the needs of strategic planning.

Overview and the iterative process

Chapter 9, by Ray Kates, gives practical advice to the planner and an overview of the process.

Planning is an iterative process where the planner must stay ahead of the game. The best advice following the successful implementation of a well thought-out strategy is to go back and start again. The successful implementation could have changed the environment in some way (it will have changed independently anyway). It will have changed a company's position in the market place, altered the resources available and developed the company culture.

The problem for the planner is living in the future and never getting any credit. Experience indicates that plans laid several years before they come to fruition are perceived by line management to have happened very quickly and with little thought. The credit for success is always claimed by someone other than the planner, which is perhaps a measure of his professionalism. The only time his work is publicly acknowledged is when the plans have gone wrong.

1 Strategic environmental appraisal

Basil Denning

Evolving a strategy

The evolution of a deliberate strategy involves three activities which interact:

- strategic environmental appraisal,
- strategic corporate appraisal,
- formulation, testing and execution of relevant strategies.

Where any of these activities is poorly performed the company runs the risk of operating with an ineffective or inappropriate strategy. The penalty for poor strategy may be liquidation or loss of autonomous control and will certainly be loss of profit and opportunity.

Defining the firm's environment

The first problem in strategic environmental appraisal is to define the firm's environment and to generate systematic information about it. Since events in the outside world are important and many are partly predictable, how can a company structure its future analysis of the mass of external events and influences so that it can make reasoned assumptions about trends vital to its future? If a satisfactory and relevant structure can be devised, on what events should information be obtained? How regularly? In what depth? By whom? At what cost? What use will be made of this information when it is gathered? What forecasting techniques can be used? With what probable margins of error?

These issues can be resolved through the questions which managers are now familiar with from experience with internal information systems. For what purpose is this information required and by whom?

It is stressed that there may be significant differences between external information required on a day-to-day basis for efficient operating and that necessary for strategic purposes. A great deal of information about short-term operating factors is normally obtained and used for everyday business but this chapter considers only the more complex problem of future strategy. There is no reason why information gathered for the ordinary course of business should be the same as that needed to resolve a company's strategic problems. Indeed a study of American companies showed that only 47 per cent of the information collected in the ordinary course of operations was of value for strategic purposes (Aguilar 1967). Nor was there any guarantee that it contained all the information relevant to the strategic issues of the company. Interrelated problems in approaching the question of strategic environmental appraisal can be set down in the form of questions.

- Within what broad structure can events, trends and factors in the environment be considered?
- How can a company determine which factors are relevant to its strategic problems?
- What methods should be used for gathering relevant information?
- What methods of forecasting would be helpful?
- Can the cost of obtaining, processing and forecasting from this information be compared with the benefit obtained?

A structure for analysis

Many structures can be used to assemble information and organise analysis for strategic appraisal. No structure is ever absolutely right or wrong, and choice of the most suitable must depend on relevance and practicality.

An example of the wide range of factors and ways of structuring them is shown in figure 1.1. It depicts the key environmental factors affecting Shell UK. The critical difficulty of environmental appraisal emerges starkly. Most of the factors have a significant impact on Shell, yet while the company may be able to exert influence over some factors, it has no control over most; this presents an inextricable problem to the planner.

Reducing this complexity into a relevant structure is started by breaking the overall environment into three broad areas:

- general factors,
- industry factors,
- competitive patterns and analyses.

General factors are those applying to all companies operating in a geographical or political area such as the EEC, the United Kingdom or the 'South East'. The principal elements to watch are demography, the economy, law and taxation and sociological patterns.

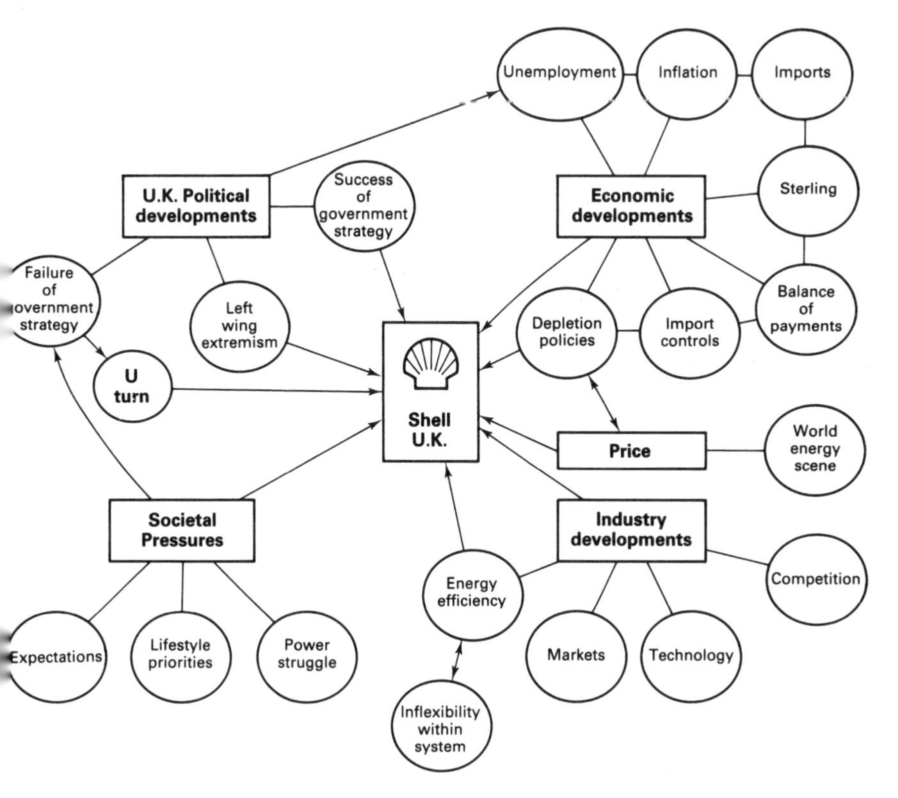

Figure 1.1 Environmental pressures *Source:* Beck (1982)

Demography A review of the basic statistics and forecasts of numbers, ages, life expectation, new family formations, sizes of household and families, and popular movements are essential background to almost all the thinking about demand and market prospects for a very wide range of businesses.
The economy General assessments of the main conventional economic parameters such as GNP, output, interest rates, world trade and inflation are essential background to most strategic decisions. Political developments and Government economic policies are critical elements for any judgement.
Law and tax The present and probable developments of commercial law, and taxation are matters for close attention. Monitoring developments in EEC law is now essential for many British companies.
Sociological pattern Sociological change is normally slow. Changing life styles and values, different patterns of work, changing aspirations of women at

work, and the different expectations of younger workers are all influences which steadily affect the fundamental economic pattern.

Turning to the industry factors which need appraisal, a more formal structure is often helpful in organising data collection, forecasting and thinking. Figure 1.2 suggests a possible structure for the packaging industry.

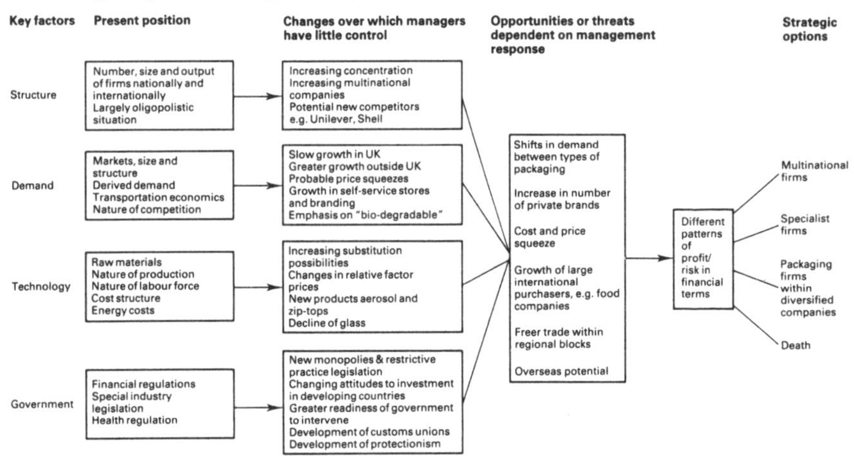

Figure 1.2 Structuring a strategic environmental analysis for the packaging industry.

Stages in the analysis

Four key factors start the analysis: structure of the industry; demand in the industry; the technological position of the industry; special legislation affecting the industry. The first task is to obtain an accurate view of the present position. Several matters regarding each factor need close attention. Some can be quantified – for example, the number, size and output of existing companies. Others may be more qualitative, such as the nature of competition and the extent to which the key competitive factors are price, delivery, credit, technical quality or some other factor.

The second stage is to use this information with other knowledge and opinion to assess future developments over which the company will have little control. For example, in the packaging industry there has been close correlation between demand for packages and gross national product. A forecast of GNP is therefore highly relevant. Similarly changes in prices of major raw materials (wood, paper, glass, tin plate, aluminium and plastic) can shift a substantial volume of demand from one type of packaging to another.

In some ways the third stage of the analysis is most critical. Once a broad picture of likely changes in the environment of the industry has been developed, these changes should be examined to see how far they represent threats, on the one hand, or opportunities on the other. To pursue our example, all companies in the packaging industry will have to respond to at least six foreseeable environmental trends, each involving threats and opportunities.

1 The tendency for customers to shift purchasing from one type of product to another in response to price changes, consumer preference and availability of new products. This is a powerful argument for not specialising in one product. Alternatively, if specialisation in one product type is chosen, it may be wise to develop a broader product base than packaging to allow for predictable change.
2 The increase in private branding may displace a substantial volume of nationally branded goods. Production may need shifting from long standard runs for a few large customers to more customers requiring smaller quantities. This may affect the economics of production and the pattern of selling arrangements.
3 A squeeze on costs and prices. To prepare for this, financial policies may need review, or diversification may be considered as a means of maintaining profitability. Alternatively, a company may increase its investment in research and development to give greater differentiation, novelty, or improved technical characteristics, so that higher margins may be maintained.
4 The increasing power and influence of multinational companies. Where a substantial volume of packaging is bought by multinational food companies, they might use their purchasing power to favour the multinational packaging company which can meet their global requirements and give larger volume discounts. This impacts on the geographical spread of factories and could offer scope to a company recognizing the trend and adapting to it.
5 Freer trade within regional blocks such as the EEC. This increases competition and the possible market to be served. Thus the geographic scope of competition is changed and the question of transportation economics needs reconsideration.
6 The industrialisation of developing countries. As this takes place new needs, both consumer and industrial, are emerging. This offers substantial growth (which is reasonably predictable by area) and opens up opportunities.

These are not the only areas of opportunity or threat. There are questions of pollution, technological advance, new entrants into the business from petrochemical companies and many others. However, the major aim of this chapter is to describe how a series of partly predictable factors can be set out and the opportunities or threats to all companies in the industry can be systematically assessed. When this process is put together with the corporate appraisal, the opportunities and threats to the individual company stand out more sharply and allow executives to make reasoned choices.

Competitive appraisal

Competitive appraisal is a large complex subject in its own right. Readers are advised to study Porter (1980). Nevertheless, this introductory chapter would be incomplete without drawing attention to two sets of ideas, the analysis of competitive structure, and the need for analysis (not just monitoring) of competitors.

The analysis of competitive structure is necessary to understand the competitive arena of business. The key forces are summarised in figure 1.3.

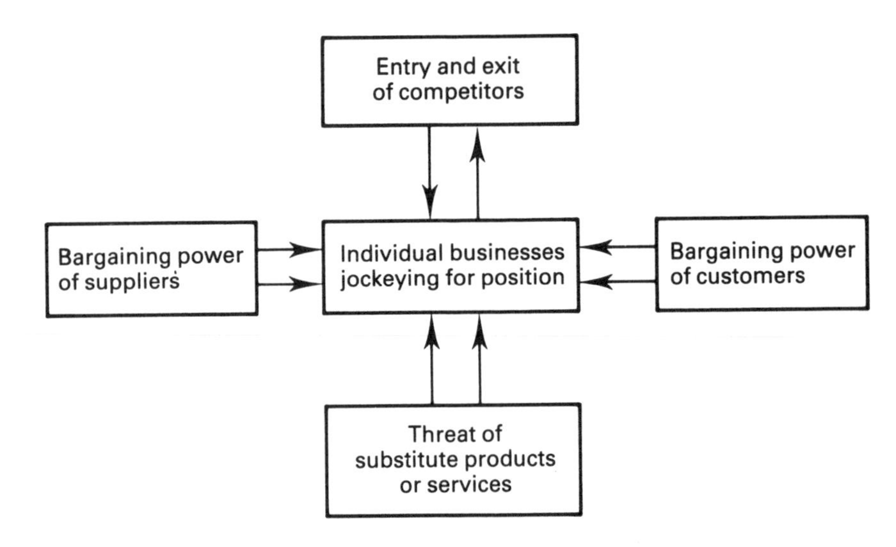

Figure 1.3 The competitive arena

The competitive arena is determined by analysis of power, present or latent. For example, the profitability of British branded food manufacturers has been drastically reduced by the high concentration of purchasing power in the hands of the five major retailing chains. By contrast, the car manufacturer has power to charge high prices for his spare parts, a quasi-monopoly position. In addition, there are two latent forces of new entrants and of substitutes. The environment of British Telecom has changed drastically with the removal of its monopoly. Changes in relative prices of aluminium, steel, glass and paper make substitution a threat to all packaging companies.

The second leg of competitive appraisal is the analysis of key competitors. Many companies monitor market shares. Too few analyse competitors seriously to find out their strong or weak points, strategy and probable intentions. An outline of the analysis required is shown in figure 1.4.

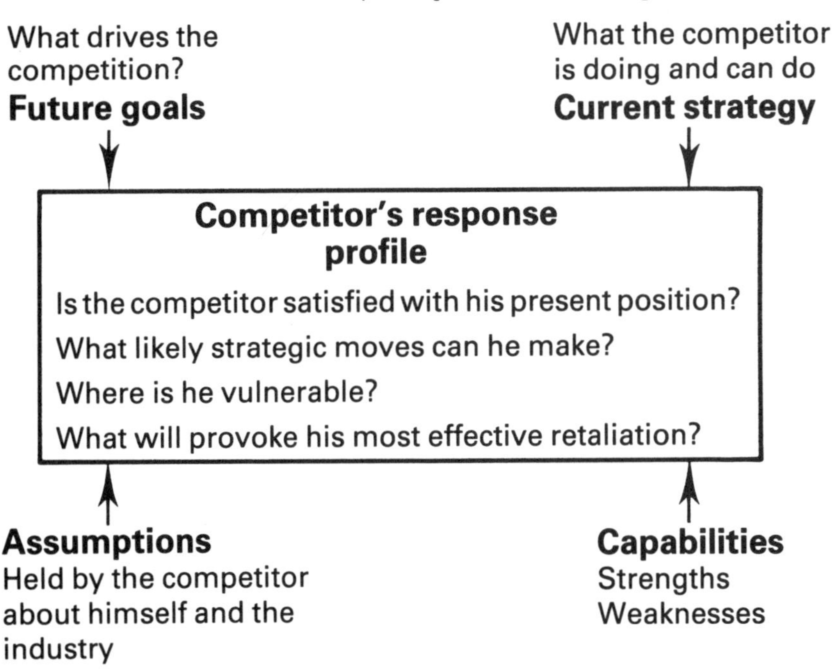

Figure 1.4 Framework for competitor analysis. *Source:* Porter (1980)

With the increasing internationalisation of large areas of business, it is imperative to identify key competitors, at home and abroad. The British motor cycle industry might not have disappeared if Japanese competition had been identified, analysed and dealt with in good time.

Which factors are relevant in strategic appraisal?

Selecting only information which is genuinely strategic is the problem in environmental appraisal. With the enormous quantity of statistics, technical reports, market data and political intelligence available, a company can be swamped with data and emerge after months of analysis with little useful information.

The need is for systematic data selection. It is useful to explore the company's sensitivity to factors on which data can be obtained and concentrate effort only on the most sensitive.

Figure 1.5 sets out examples of external factors of different sensitivity to companies in two industries, a manufacturer of telephone equipment and an integrated oil company. Consider gross national product and government capital spendings: demand for oil is acutely sensitive to changes in gross national product whereas, in the short run, the demand for telephone equipment is not.

In contrast, the level of government-authorised capital spending is a critical element in demand for communications equipment but is not a major determinant of demand for oil. This simple example of exploring external sensitivities, some quantititive, some qualitative, illustrates the use of an important method of choosing factors on which to spend effort.

	A major manufacturer of telephone equipment	An integrated oil company
GNP	Medium	High
Government capital spending	Very high	Low
Technical change	Very high	Medium/low (except for electric car)
Sociological change	Very high (communication habits)	Very high (private car movements)
Environmental pollution	Low	High
Political risks Middle East	Low	High

Figure 1.5 Examples of comparative environmental sensitivities

In my experience many businessmen are unable to make the link between a specific change in the environment and their business. Some companies have made significant studies of these relationships and an excellent treatise is given by Chandler and Cockle (1982). Few companies, however, will be able to afford the effort suggested in that book, and a 'poor man's approach' of testing the sensitivity of his business to significant environmental variables can produce helpful insights and results.

Methods of gathering information

The executive's next problem is to choose how he will obtain the relevant information and determine the costs he will incur in obtaining it. An enormous volume of data, comment, gossip and reports may have something useful to contribute to an understanding of the environment.

Little effective research has been done on this problem but Aguilar (1967) reports how a small group of American companies obtained external information, the use they made of it, how it was disseminated in the company, and its value in strategic or operational problems. A fairly haphazard state of affairs is normal. Aguilar suggests that some order can be obtained by classifying scanning approaches into the four modes set out in figure 1.6.

Undirected viewing	General exposure with no specific purpose, e.g. newspapers, general journals, magazines.
Conditioned viewing	Directed exposure to a more or less clearly identified area of information plus readiness to assume its possible importance, e.g. trade journals, lunching in the City, attending a conference.
Informal search	Limited and unstructured effort to obtain specific information e.g. telephoning small group of contacts.
Formal search	Deliberate effort to receive particular information e.g. market survey, economic forecasting model, needs research, acquisition search.

Figure 1.6 Modes of scanning environmental factors

These four classifications represent the levels of effort which may be devoted to different types of environmental information and provide a framework for choosing the level. They range from 'undirected viewing' i.e. general exposure to newspapers and journals at minimal expense, to the 'formal search' including specially commissioned market research, normally an expensive choice.

In choosing how much effort to put into scanning different factors it is helpful to draw together the structure of environmental appraisal and the concept of sensitivity. All areas which should be scanned emerge as significant in the appraisal of the present position and the forecast changes over which the company has no control. Above the minimum level of undirected viewing, a company should devote more effort to those factors to which it is most sensitive. It makes sense for an integrated oil company to build econometric forecasting models to provide regular forecasts of the gross national products of industrial nations. However, the telephone equipment manufacturer may feel that conditioned viewing, in this case a critical review of published economic forecasts, is adequate. Similarly, he may spend a substantial amount on formal search to examine technical and scientific developments in electronics. This would not be justified for the oil company.

In deciding on the appropriate level of effort and how to gather information, distinguish between information needed for short term operations and that for strategic appraisal. All companies have enormous amounts of information reaching them every day from the outside world, but much of it is relevant only to operational decisions. Examples are the rumour of a new promotion by a competitor, comparisons of wage and salary rates between firms and competitors' anticipated price changes. Much of the information required for strategic purposes, however, is of a different order – proposals for new legislation, news of a competitor company looking for a buyer, the report of a new process being introduced by a competitor which will reduce his operating costs. It is important to help operating personnel to develop perception to identify strategic information and to transmit it to those concerned with strategic problems. In most companies, positive efforts need to be made to explain to management what is strategic and to encourage reporting of this sort of information.

Choosing forecasting methods

Companies make individual forecasts on selected matters. This is not the place to examine the techniques of forecasting but it is appropriate to consider some of the problems of forecasting environmental factors.

It is important to define the purpose of the forecast. A pioneer in the field of technological forecasting (Quinn 1967) wrote:

> 'To be useful, technological forecasts do not necessarily need to predict the precise form technology will take in a given application at some specific future date. Like any other forecasts, their purpose is simply to help evaluate the probability and significance of various possible future developments so that managers can make better decisions'.

It is worth remembering that environmental forecasts are used to provide assumptions on which planning can take place. Forecasting to provide planning assumptions, however, is different from forecasting production requirements or to inform shareholders. The degree of accuracy required is different. It may be considerably more valuable to forecast that over the next ten years the industry is likely to shift to an oligopolistic structure with four or five dominant firms and a selection of smaller specialist firms, than to forecast gross national product to plus or minus two per cent five years ahead. Again, the accuracy needed can be determined by applying the sensitivity tests described earlier.

Because accuracy is not too critical, many companies rely on published forecasts rather than develop their own. Using these calls for considerable expertise; it is a different task from that of the working forecaster. It needs an ability to question assumptions, to examine for coherence, to compare differences with other forecasts and to apply judgement. Many forecasting services are available, some on a regular basis such as the major institutional economic forecasts, others more specialised and periodic on specific market areas, technologies, and sociological developments. If you are feeling really ambitious you can rent the Treasury model of the economy and enter your own variables!

Many key environmental variables are not quantitative in nature. For example, a critical forecasting area for an integrated oil company is the political situation in the Middle East and the power plays within OPEC. While the effects of certain actions can be quantified, the forecast of probable developments and of their timing means sifting expert opinion and establishing probabilities.

Finally, any forecast for a long period should be approached with scepticism. Most forecasts are built up on a substantial data base, an explicit or implicit model, and assumptions which incorporate a substantial degree of continuity of most recent trends, modified by judgement. They almost never incorporate sudden shifts or discontinuities. In some cases this may not be significant. For example, forecasts of the numbers of children entering secondary school in ten years time can be treated with considerable confidence. The children have already been born and the effect of estimating errors in deaths, emigration and immigration will be small. Contrast this with forecasting the price of oil a mere five years ahead. Evaluating demand is difficult enough, but the effects of war in the Middle East, blockades of the Arabian Gulf or producers leaving OPEC are likely to outweigh the effect of conventional supply-demand analyses.

'Scenarios' and 'surprises'

Two approaches to this difficulty are worth mentioning. The first is to use scenarios rather than forecasts. The most vigorous exponent of scenarios is the Shell Group and their approach is described by Zentner (1982) and Higgins (1980).

Essentially, Shell says that forecasts are not only inaccurate, they are positively dangerous because they give a false sense of security to decision makers. Forecasts which turn out wrong will be used as excuses by managers whose decisions turn out badly. Instead, Shell makes no single forecast of the major environmental variables. It draws up, with the extensive use of models, pictures of at least three 'possible worlds'. No probability is attached to any of them but managers are asked to test their plans and proposals against each scenario. Shell believes this has provoked better strategic thinking throughout the company and has increased flexibility.

Drawing up scenarios of this complexity, however, is expensive and initally confusing to decision makers. A cheaper and frequently effective approach is to identify against a base forecast, three or four specific 'surprises'. For example: if the base forecast of interest rates suggests a range of between 10% and 12%, it may be worth inserting a 'surprise' possibility that interest rates will rise to 16% at some point in the planning period, and require strategic decision makers to examine the robustness of their proposals if this 'surprise' should develop.

Costs and benefits of systematic environmental appraisal

It would be comforting if this chapter could end with convincing evidence that a systematic approach to the strategic analysis of the environment pays direct cash dividends. I know of no studies of this type and would hesitate to accept their conclusions if they exist. One needs only to be reminded of the complete failure of the German general staff in the Second World War to use the priceless information obtained by 'Cicero' about future Allied intentions to realise the difficulty. Information obtained from any source must be absorbed and believed and acted upon. In the Cicero case, the information was not absorbed because it contradicted other information arising from a separate and 'private' source. Many individuals may absorb information but not really believe that it has value, especially if it conflicts with conventional wisdom or practice. Even if it is believed and acted upon, there is no guarantee that the action will be wise. It would be imprudent therefore to expect too solid a result from any cost benefit research study.

Perhaps it is wiser to return to first principles. The basis of the argument for a more systematic and professional approach to any management problem is not that you will ensure a 'right' answer, but that you increase the probability of success of a series of decisions over time. From first principles, observation and experience, it is argued that knowledge of the environment is necessary to any company in deciding how it will conduct itself in the future. Obtaining knowledge of the environment can be carried out haphazardly or systematically. A systematic approach means that the type of information needed is determined from some structured picture of the environment and efforts are made to obtain information on all the factors within the structure. Since finding information takes time and money, the level of effort and cost devoted to different types of information are examined together with the accuracy needed for the purpose in mind. Whether the benefit justifies the cost can then be determined by subjective assessment. Whether relevant information is being passed from technical, marketing and financial executives to the areas where it may be helpful for strategic decisions can also be assessed.

These are the essentials of a systematic approach. It is likely to ensure that a company is not missing out on vital knowledge of the environment and is reasonably well informed about the key external factors affecting it. The company is more likely to have an effective grasp of its opportunities and threats and so take better decisions about the future than one which relies solely on haphazard methods. In practice, few companies of any size are completely haphazard. They cannot afford to be. Nevertheless, most companies can improve the probability of making wise strategic decisions and using their external information gathering resources more effectively if they use the systematic approach described in this chapter.

2 Strengths and weaknesses of companies

David Hussey

Introduction

Strengths and weakness analysis can be approached from a number of directions. The task is amenable to consultancy, self analysis by task force, and bottom-up participative approaches. Some firms tackle the task themselves Others bring in outsiders to help keep the analysis objective.

The biggest pitfall is the most common. Too often the corporate plan presents its strengths and weakness analysis in platitudes, or omits information of strategic importance. This is often because the analytical framework is unsound, or it may be because the behavioural implications of the analysis are ignored. The purpose of this chapter is to remedy these defects. It begins with a framework for analysis, and ends with approaches designed to remove some of the behavioural issues. In between are some other relevant concepts which will help make sense of this complex task.

Analysing your industry

The framework for analysis should be the competitive strengths and weaknesses of the firm in the context of the industry in which it operates. The issues identified will be both relevant and strategic in nature.

In this analysis the aim is to examine the factors which cause the intensity of competitive rivalry in the industry, and the way in which industry profits are affected by the relative power and influence of other factors in the drama – the suppliers to and buyers from the industry. Add to this the pressure on profits caused by substitutes, and the nature and strength of exit and entry barriers to the industry, and we have a strategic framework within which the firm can be placed.

The credit for much of the original work of drawing these concepts into a usable framework belongs to Porter (1980). Almost all of the concepts were derived from the practical application of basic economic theory, and the new dimension has been to pull these together in one coherent approach. Figure 1.3 in Chapter 1 illustrates the concepts of industry structure analysis.

The five basic elements, which can be termed the competitive forces, working on any industry are:

1 **Competition between firms in the industry**
Inter-firm competition in such factors as price, advertising, service and quality.

2 **Competition from substitute products**
At best substitutes may put a ceiling on the prices and profits of the industry. At worst they may remove the whole market.

3 **Bargaining power of suppliers**
The relative strength of suppliers vis-à-vis firms in the industry will affect the extent to which the industry firm is forced to accept price increases. Implicit in the power structure is the likelihood of the supplier entering the industry as a competitor.

4 **Bargaining power of customers**
Relative power of the customer will affect prices and service levels of the industry. Where customer power is strong, there may also be the threat of backward integration.

5 **Entry and exit of competitors**
The ease of movement in and out of the industry will affect the competitive behaviour of firms in the industry.

Analysing these factors will show why some industries are more profitable than others, and who controls the industry. It provides a foundation for the application of strategic portfolio analysis techniques, enables the critical success factors for the industry to be established, and enables judgement on whether a particular factor is a strength or a weakness.

Much of what is good or bad about the company can only be interpreted against the competitive structure of the industry. Is a market share of 10% a strength or a weakness? It depends. In a mature industry, where there are few competitors, and the firm has third position after competitors with 60% and 30%, a 10% share may be a weakness, too small for long term viable operation. However, in a fragmented industry in the growth phase of the life cycle, 10% may be the highest share and a sign that the company is moving ahead and will come out well in the shake-out phase of the life cycle.

Take another example. Is an annual 20% productivity improvement a strength or a weakness? Again it depends on what competitors' costs are doing, whether they are improving faster, and who is in the lead. Interpretation is only possible in the context of the industry. In the mid-seventies the most efficient British motor cycle producer had an output of 18 motor cycles per man year. Hardly any productivity increase would have been good enough to match the most efficient Honda plant with an output of 350 motor cycles per man year.

In undertaking industry structure analysis it is necessary to move from the simple concept of figure 1.3 and to identify the actual structure of the particular industry. Figure 2.1 shows how complex this may be and is drawn from the viewpoint of a grower of fruit and vegetables. If we were looking at the industry from the viewpoint of a manufacturer of glasshouses we would be interested in his key suppliers (for example, glass, aluminium), but may not wish to study that portion of the industry beyond the grower.

My experience in charting the structure of an industry with clients is that they are usually well informed about the particular channels they use, and are often ill informed about channels they do not use. Seeing the total picture is an essential prerequisite of judging strengths and weaknesses.

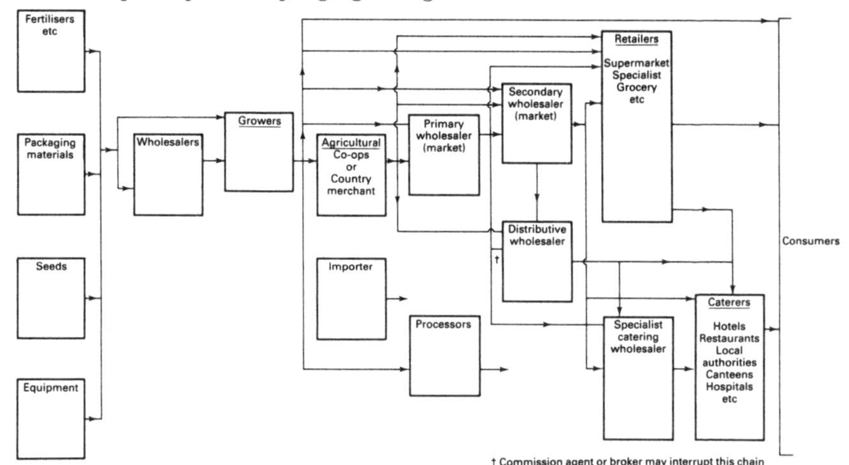

Figure 2.1 Structure of the fruit and vegetable industry, UK

General principles behind industry structure analysis: competitors

The following general principles of industry structure analysis summarise many points made by Porter (1980). They are general tendencies rather than inexorable laws, and of course need to be considered as a whole.

1 As the number of competitors increases, or as they become more equal in size and power there is a tendency for contention to grow in the industry.

The influx of new competitors tends to lead to competitive reactions by the existing firms in the industry, as they try to keep their customers and prevent the new firms from gaining a foothold. The impact of this may be modified by the growth rate in the market; it will be magnified if growth slows.

An industry also tends to be more aggressively competitive when it consists of a number of firms of roughly equal size, so that no one firm is in a dominating position and all are scrambling to defend and expand market share.

2 Contention increases as growth rates slow

If a market is growing fast, competitors may meet their own growth targets without changing market share. When rates decline, whether because of short-term recession or long-term trends, competitors can only meet their objectives by taking share from others. This leads to more aggressive behaviour. However, note that a high growth rate tends to attract new competitors to an industry.

3 Competition increases when the product is perishable or difficult or costly to store.

There is an obvious incentive to sell quickly when a product is perishable (such as a seat on a train, a professional service, or fresh produce), and this tends to lead to a more competitive environment than when the product is durable. Similarly, if a product is costly to store, there will also be pressure on firms to dispose of it quickly.

4 Where fixed costs are a high proportion of total costs, or where there is a potentially large investment in dedicated assets, there will be a tendency for competition to become more aggressive.

Particularly in the short to medium term, competitors will be tempted into price competition when supply and demand are out of balance. Then industries such as petrochemicals find it more profitable to operate at any level of price which covers variable cost and makes some contribution to fixed costs, rather than temporarily cease trading. Similarly, if there is no clear alternative use for a specialised investment, such as a petrochemical plant, competitors will tend to continue to operate it rather than write the assets off.

5 Competition increases the more standardised and less differentiated the product, reaching a peak as it nears commodity status.

Product differentiation rarely removes competition, but does reduce its ferocity. The protection is greatest when the buyer would incur extra costs if he changed to a different firm (e.g. machinery modification, formula changes). Products which have no differentiation, that is commodities, have to fight for sales on all fronts.

General principles behind industry structure analysis: suppliers

1 Suppliers will tend to try to influence the growth of the purchasing industry when it accounts for a large proportion of their total output. They will also be vulnerable to margin pressure by their purchasers unless there are countervailing influences. The availability of competing substitute products will tend to reduce the power of suppliers and increase purchasing industry profitability.

Suppliers are vulnerable where one industry takes a very high proportion of their output, and even more so if that industry is made up of few firms. In this situation they will often take an interest in the markets served by their customers, taking action where possible to expand them (e.g. packaging industry).

2 The relative size of supplying and purchasing firms is also a factor which affects profitability. Additional power over margins tends to be held by suppliers when supplier firms are considerably larger than purchasing firms, because it is known that they have the resources to override difficulties. The converse applies when the relative size positions are reversed (e.g. think of the power a retailer such as Marks & Spencer has over its suppliers).

3 Suppliers may increase their bargaining power if they can demonstrate a credible threat to integrate forward. Conditions for forward integration by suppliers may occur when:

- the purchasing industry has a higher rate of profitability than the supplier industry,
- the volume of business in the hands of any one supplier reaches the scale of operations which would be needed to open a plant,
- there would be economies brought about through integration,
- the purchasing industry acts in a way that thwarts the development of the suppliers (e.g. refusal to take its new products),
- there are no insuperable entry barriers.

It is worth noting that suppliers do not have to integrate forwards to gain influence over margins. There need only be a credible threat that they might.

4 On the other hand the purchasing industry can reduce the power of the suppliers if it can offer a credible threat to integrate backwards. Some of the conditions are the converse of 3 above.

General principles behind industry structure analysis: buyers

1 The ability of the industry to raise prices is inhibited when the buying industry has a low value added. This is particularly true when the buyer faces an elastic demand curve, which prevents him passing on cost increases, while the low value added leaves few internal opportunities for productivity increases.

2 The power of the buyers is higher the more the industry is dominated by powerful customers, the fewer the numbers of buying firms, and the greater their percentage purchases from the industry. The power of the buyer decreases as the supplying industry becomes more concentrated.

General principles behind industry structure analysis: entry and exit barriers

1 Barriers to entry have been defined (Bannock, Baxter and Rees, 1979) as:

> 'Features of technological or economic conditions of a market which raise the costs of firms already in the market or otherwise make new entry difficult. For example, a high degree of product differentiation creates a barrier to entry since a new product might need a great deal spent on advertising and sales promotion to overcome the loyalty of consumers to existing brands. Similarly, economies of scale in the industry may require the new firm to enter at a very large scale of output, if it is not to suffer a disadvantage. But the need to capture a large part of the market may cause a fall in prices and profits and make entry unprofitable. We would expect the nature of barriers to entry of an industry to be an important determinant of profits earned in the industry. Hence, with very low barriers, we would expect profits in the long run to approach normal profits. On the other hand, high entry barriers will strengthen monopoly power and may permit high profits to be made. Other important sources of entry barriers are patents, exclusive dealing contracts with suppliers or distributors, and vertical integration. On the other hand, entry barriers will be less effective when there is rapid expansion in demand, or technological change'.

2 Exit barriers are the factors which tie a firm to the industry and make it difficult or impossible for it to leave. Where they occur, the firm will hang on, trading as best it can, and depressing profits in the industry.

Exit barriers may be around the need to write off specialised assets for which there is no buyer, particular contracts, or legal requirements which make it costly to meet severance payments to employees. There may also be government pressure on the firm to stay in the business.

General principles behind industry structure analysis: substitutes

The threat of new substitutes is similar to that of a new entry to the industry, except that a substitute may be better or cheaper than existing products. In thinking about substitutes, the firm should also consider the likelihood of substitutes impacting its buyer's market.

Analysing your company

The second analytical approach, which should be interpreted in the framework of the industry analysis, is usually referred to in the literature as the corporate appraisal or position audit. Much of the inspiration for the approaches I have used comes from Drucker (1964). This book could be used as a handbook for anyone who has to approach this task, and its age in no way reduces the validity of its message:

> 'The basic business analysis starts with an examination of the business as it is now, the business as it has been bequeathed to us by the decisions, actions and results of the past. We need to see the hard skeleton, the basic stuff that is the economic structure. We need to see the relationship, and inter-relations of resources and results, of efforts and achievements, of revenues and costs'.

The appraisal can be conducted by the company itself, but is likely to be more effective if some degree of outside help is sought. This is partly the question of objectives mentioned earlier. It is partly because an appraisal frequently has to challenge the conventions of the accounting system (particularly in firms using an absorption system). It is also because managers within a firm often share a common perception of the boundaries of their problems, and solve them logically within this boundary. Where the perception is wrong, the logic of the solution may be destroyed. In an article where I argued this point in greater detail (Hussey 1984) I likened this to the certainty in the Middle Ages that the world was flat. Within this perceptual boundary logical decisions were made, which eventually were to prove wrong.

An obvious starting point for the corporate appraisal is the company's historical pattern of performance: trends in profit, sales, capital employed, and then all the ratios that may be derived from these to measure efficiently. To make sense the analysis should be broken down by subsidiary companies, departments, or areas of performance: see Figure 2.2.

One useful presentation is a series of charts based on the standard ROI (Return on Investment) chart. These illustrate sales, direct costs and contribution by activity areas, product areas, and if possible customer types, and show the balance sheet under the same headings: see Figure 2.3.

Two of Drucker's points are worth stressing. First, apportioned costs usually misrepresent reality. Secondly, activity areas should be classified by future significance. He suggests: 'today's breadwinners, tomorrow's breadwinners, productive specialties, development products, failures, yesterday's breadwinners, repair jobs, unnecessary specialties, unjustified specialties, investments in managerial ego, cinderellas (or sleepers)'.

It is around the sources of profit that questions should be asked about rationalisation opportunities. Could resources be merged for greater effectiveness? Are there too many products? Are there too many variants of package size?

By this stage of the study it is possible to see some of the strategic vulnerabilities in the firm's position. If a very high proportion of profit is contributed by one product or business activity there may not necessarily be a weakness but there is certainly cause for concern. Add to this the information already obtained in the industry structure analysis, and it is possible to see the degree of dependency on a few buyers or suppliers.

Attention should next be turned to manufacturing, looking not only at the competitiveness of production processes and methods, but also at the conflicts present in the way production is organised. For example a factory which tries to use the same machinery for a mass-produced product and occasional specials is likely to find that it has problems. Skinner (1978) is recommended for those who wish further information and relatively new thinking in this important corporate activity.

Organisation and the management structure should be included in the study. This would cover the competence of key people, the age profile of the management team, the organisational structure and the corporate systems. (For further reading see Galbraith and Nathanson, 1978).

There are various ways of pulling together the results of the corporate appraisal. One which I have used is given as an example in the appendix to this chapter. It is important to note that this form of summary presentation must be supported by a dossier of evidence.

									Utilisation of resources					
Product	Current annual sales (£000)	% of total sales	Sales growth past 5 years	Market prospects	Competitors	Brand share	True profit contr. (£000)	% Total profit contr.	% fixed assets	% working capital	% R&D time	% Prod. capacity	% sales force time	Remarks
A (56 variations)	3000	50	2% p.a.	−10% p.a.	Strong and strengthening	40%	300	75	60	45	5	40	95	Present breadwinner doubtful future
B (3 variations)	600	10	15% p.a.	+25% p.a.	Weak-new competition probable	75%	4	1	5	10	25	12	1	Future breadwinner Profits can be improved by a process just developed
C (1 variation)	300	5	New product	+10% p.a.	Nil-will change within two years	100%	60	15	2	4	30	10	3	High profitability will not continue once product under competitive attack
D (30 variations)	30	1	Nil	+25% p.a.	Many competitors	10%	−4	−1	10	1	12	10	Nil	No future for this product
E (10 variations)	30	1	+2½% p.a.	Not known	No information	Not known	4	1	1	1	Nil	1	Nil	

Figure 2.2 Product contribution and resources

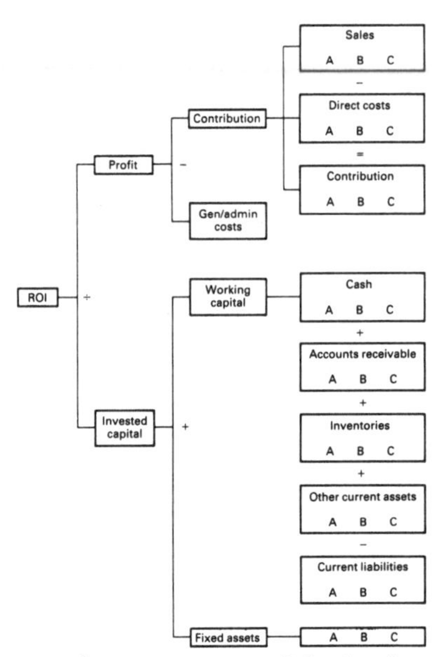

Figure 2.3 ROI chart to show structure of the business

Bottom-up analysis

Both the industry analysis and the corporate appraisal are analytical, and the evaluation has to be carefully structured to give the best results. An alternative, and less analytical, method is to follow a behavioural route, asking people throughout the organisation to give their views of the company's strengths and weaknesses. These are collated. To be most effective it is best to bring participants together in groups of no more than 12 people to gain some consensus over items and their importance. This process is repeated several times, and eventually a master list can be derived.

The main advantage of this method is that it involves a great number of people in the planning process. Its main failing is that it is not necessarily objective and may miss out important points because those involved share common perceptual frontiers.

Another behavioural tool can be used to encourage participation in strengths and weakness analysis. This is equilibrium analysis, a problem-related approach derived from the forcefield concepts of the behaviouralists and described in more detail in the next section.

In most organisations there is value in considering a behavioural method to complement the analysis. The style of the organisation and its structure affect the degree to which this is possible, while the situation the company faces will determine whether it is desirable. These first two points are self evident, but the third requires some explanation. A company in severe crisis usually needs fast and incisive decision making, and cannot afford the time to obtain maximum participation. In these circumstances quick assessments are needed.

Equilibrium analysis

Many attempts at analysing strengths and weaknesses, particularly those which involve the managers, result in unusable data. The typical end product is a shopping list of rather general statements which are usually difficult to evaluate. Issues are often exaggerated. It is rare that action results because of these attempts.

The equilibrium approach is intended for use in group sessions. Its objectives are:

- To achieve a common understanding of strengths and weaknesses.
- To identify strengths as well as weaknesses.
- To decide priorities for corrective action.
- To identify corrective action.

An example of the approach is shown in Figure 2.4. It is a very simple concept which can be taught to any group in a matter of minutes. The horizontal line represents the present state of anything that is to be studied such as labour turnover rates, market position, cost structures, or profitability. Focus should be given by posing a question such as 'Why is our market share 15%?' The base line then represents the current stage – market share 15%. It is as high as 15% because certain positive features support it. It is as low as 15% because certain negative features hold it down.

The trick is to get the meeting to identify these two groups of factors, writing them at the top and bottom of the diagram, across the page. If too many weaknesses are identified attention can be changed to strengths with a remark such as 'Now I can't understand why you have any market share at all'. If too many strengths come up one can ask why market share has not risen to 50%.

Successful use of the approach needs a group of people who know the situation, and some preparation for the meeting by an analyst who has looked at the factual base available. He should be prepared to challenge (e.g. if the group insists that a plus factor is the firm's reputation, whereas market research shows that it has none, the factual position should over-ride the impression).

The next step is to rate the relative significance of the factors identified. This is the reason for the scaling on the vertical line.

Figure 2.4 illustrates what the completed diagram might look like at the end of the meeting.

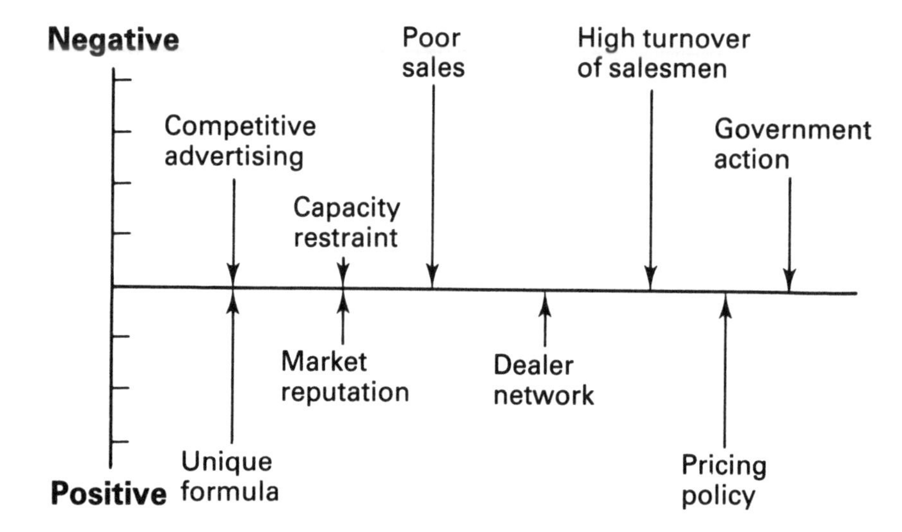

Baseline condition = market share of 15%

Figure 2.4 Examples of equilibrium analysis

Once the information is displayed it is possible to use it to consider:

- Would the position best be improved by strengthening a positive factor or removing a negative one?
- Are there any factors which cannot be altered by the firm, and which should not receive more attention?
- What can be done about the really important factors?

The equilibrium approach could be used again if it was decided to tackle high salesman turnover, and used to try to identify the factors which attract salesmen to the firm, and those that cause them to leave.

SWOT

This is not a term of abuse, but an example of one of several acronyms which describe what are basically similar presentations of the final list of strengths and weaknesses. SWOT stands for Strengths, Weaknesses, Opportunities, Threats, and in common with most of these approaches combines assessments of internal factors with those derived from external sources in the market and the business environment. Although many of these external factors are beyond the scope of this chapter, the idea that the corporate appraisal should draw on them is worth stressing. Of course anyone undertaking industry structure

analysis will have been forced to look outside the firm towards the market. Adding the dimension of the overall environment is no great extension of thinking. Other acronyms are:
SOFT (S.R.I.)*: strength, opportunity, fault, threat.
WOTS UP (Steiner): weakness, opportunity, threat, strength, underlying planning.

In some cases the authors suggest a method of presentation, which is useful. Others offer a philosophy of either self-analysis by managers, or, in the case of the Stanford Research Institute's* approach, a defined procedure for causing this self-analysis to happen.

It obviously makes sense to get managers to consider the strengths and weaknesses of their position. However these methods carry some dangers which should be appreciated:

(a) They may encourage a superficial approach. The presentation of the information should follow careful analysis, and not be a substitute for it.
(b) The temptation to come up with platitudes has to be avoided.
(c) It is often difficult to make sure the conclusions do influence the plans.
(d) There is a tendency for strengths to be underrated and most emphasis to be placed on weaknesses.

Nevertheless, there is potential value in the methods. Figure 2.5 shows the SWOT form of presentation which I have found useful. It should be noted that this can be used at corporate level, (although it may be inappropriate at this level for a complex multi-national), and at the level of divisions or products. Often the value of the SWOT approach lies in the presentation and communication rather than in the analysis itself.

Critical skills analysis

This is a completely different approach useful as an additional tool, adding more insight to the others. It follows a simple concept. In any business there are a few things that have to be done really well in order to achieve success. There may be no more than six to twelve key items. Get those right and you get the business right.

If the critical skills can be identified for a particular business it becomes possible to see whether the company is deficient in any of those skills. For example a recent study suggested that the following success factors applied:

Automotive industry	*Supermarket*
Styling product mix	
Quality dealer systems	Inventory
Cost control	Sales promotion
Meeting energy standards	Price

Source: Rockhart (1979)

Critical skills analysis is useful for finding gaps, or for ensuring that a new business strategy is properly thought out. The concept of six to twelve key skills may be a little theoretical: the question 'what do we have to be good at in order to succeed?' is very pertinent.

In practice, I have found it useful to establish the critical skills for each of the business types identified in the industry analysis diagram, and to use a version of this diagram to present the information. In Figure 2.1 for example it is clear that the critical skills required to be an importer are different from those of a travelling wholesaler (who sells from the lorry to retailers). Understanding these differences is important to anyone trying to operate in this industry, whether trying to gain insight into his own operations or those of competitors.

Strength	**Weakness**
Opportunity	**Threat**
Summary of major strategic implications	

Figure 2.5 The SWOT approach

Appendix to Chapter 2

A method of summarising the corporate appraisal

Part 1 – Weaknesses/Limiting Factors

Factor	*Strategic Implications*
1. *Management*	1. *Management*
(a) Chief Executive age 65, no obvious successor.	*(a)* Recruitment, merger, or sale of business. Main priority for action.
(b) Middle Management can be graded as: % of Managers Weak 50 Mediocre 10 Good 40	*(b) i)* Recruitment in weak areas. *ii)* Management development and training. *iii)* Reorganisation.
(c) The company undertakes no management development or training of any kind.	*(c)* Investigate feasibility of systematic approach to management development.
(d) Organisational lines and relationships are undefined. No organisation chart exists.	*(d)* Implementation of the reorganisation proposals (recommended in separate report).
(e) Marketing manager 60, has been seriously ill and is unlikely to be able to cope with change or expansion.	*(e)* See reorganisational proposals. Problem must be solved if company to develop.
2. *Marketing*	2. *Marketing*
(a) 75% of profits emanate from product A. Market declining at 10% per year. Market share under attack from competitors with superior products.	*(a) i)* Reduce dependence on this one product – see separate report. *ii)* Examine market strategy to seek improvement (see also 2b). *iii)* Improve product. *iv)* Cost reduction – value analysis, process development.
(b) Advertising and promotional expenditure is haphazard, dispersed over various types of media and methods, and is without any form of follow-up to measure impact or effect.	*(b) i)* Relate to new marketing strategy. *ii)* Cease promotion through sponsorship – saving £50,000 per year. *iii)* Market research to measure impact of current advertising.

(c) Fifty-six variations of pack or label of product A.

(c) Reduce variety to ten, saving £30,000 per year in packaging, warehousing, finance, and production costs.

(d) Fifteen products (one hundred variations) account for 12% of sales and contribute no profit. Ten of these are in a loss situation (two make a loss on variable costs).

(d) i) Cease production, redeploy resources on twelve products.
ii) Develop marketing plan to exploit three products in growth markets.

(e) 45% of order transactions account for 2½% of sales. There is a loss on these transactions.

(e) Review minimum order sizes, price structures, and physical distribution methods.

Part 2 – Strengths

---

1. *Management*
   (a) Skilful and competent production management.

1. *Management*
   (a) Exploit in managing new product production and cost reduction on existing products.

2. *People*
   (a) Strong sense of loyalty to company, and morale high in factories (although not high in marketing).

2. *People*
   (a) i) Make best use of this in reorganising for change.
   ii) Ensure that managerial style encourages these feelings.

3. *Marketing*
   (a) Strong image among consumers for service. Quality image remains although suffering from impact of competitors' better products.

3. *Marketing*
   (a) Transfer to other products.

3 Capital structure, gearing and 'going public'

William Hyde

The mix of capital

As the possible paths the company might follow are studied, the availability or shortage of money represents a limiting factor on them and a financial strategy will have to be developed. This essential element in the company's overall corporate strategy must be designed to ensure the provision of adequate finance for the company's needs. Without sufficient funds a company cannot safely expand as quickly as it might wish; lack of funds is the most common cause of business failure, and can lead to the collapse of profitable and growing firms as well as those in decline. On the other hand, a permanent surplus of funds, while less damaging, is uneconomic.

Having decided on the amount of funds needed by the company, management has to decide how this total sum should be provided. A company's operations are usually financed by money drawn from a variety of sources; in what proportions should they contribute to the total? What should the 'capital structure' of the company be?

In some respects this question is similar to those concerning choice of personnel and assets. In selecting employees management tries to arrange a balance of skills which best suits the requirements of the total tasks to be achieved, and it decides what property, plant and material are needed for the operation of the business. Efficiency (which embraces relative costs) and risk are taken into account. Similarly, the company's finances should be arranged in such a way that its objectives are achieved as efficiently and economically as possible, within the limitations set by the degree of risk considered acceptable.

Main sources of finance

It is necessary at this stage to list the main categories of corporate capital and debt, and to comment briefly on their characteristics.

Equity capital;
Preference capital;
Long-term loans;
Short-term loans;

Equity capital

All businesses carry some element of risk; that profits may be well below the level expected, that losses may be made, that things will go so badly that the business will have to be wound up. This being the case it is unrealistic for a company to expect to obtain the finance it needs entirely on fixed-interest terms. No lender of funds is willing to accept the full risks of a business for a fixed annual return. Before a company can expect to obtain a proportion of its funds on fixed-interest terms it must establish a base of share capital which will bear the major part of the risk. This risk capital is provided by the owners of the ordinary shares, and comprises the funds which have been subscribed by the ordinary shareholders, plus accumulated reserves (or less any deficit carried forward).

The ordinary shareholders rank for dividends last after all due payments out of profits have been made. Similarly, equity capital ranks last for repayment in the event, say, of a compulsory liquidation. It therefore bears the higher risk. Prior-ranking finance, being less risky, can be attracted on fixed-payment terms.

Equity capital is thus an essential part of the funds of any company, and additional finance from this source arises from annual retentions of earnings and from new issues of shares.

Most companies retain each year some proportion of their net earnings after tax, although in the last decade or so this proportion has declined. In addition, since depreciation provisions are part of the annual cash flow they can be regarded as funds in effect 'made available' to the company by the shareholders. Even though they do not feature on the capital and liability side of a balance sheet (but are netted off the assets), they are usually an important source of funds over which management has control, and they need to be taken into account in a company's financial plan.

A limited company can also invite subscriptions for additional ordinary shares, and as will be discussed later, one of the main reasons for obtaining a public quotation for its shares is to enable the company to approach the general public for equity capital.

Preference shares

Preference shares form part of the share capital of a limited company; the holders are therefore as much members of the company as are the ordinary shareholders. They are normally entitled to a fixed annual distribution, paid out of the net earnings of a company and ranking before any ordinary dividends.

Preference capital provides part of the 'borrowing base' of a company; it provides some of the security required by creditors. If profits fall, preference dividends are omitted before the company contemplates defaulting on its interest payments. If there is a winding-up, creditors must be paid in full before preference shareholders can receive any distribution.

Long-term loans

Basically, there are three types of loan capital which rank in ascending order. They are unsecured loans, floating charge debentures and fixed charge debentures.

1 Unsecured loans
In a liquidation, unsecured loans rank equally with non-preferential creditors of a limited company. Any creditor who has a charge on any of the assets, e.g. a mortgage, ranks for payment out of the assets charged in advance of the unsecured creditors. On the issue of an unsecured loan stock, the normal requirement is that a trust deed or loan should be executed setting out the terms and containing a number of clauses setting out particular rights and restrictions, often including a covenant by the company under which charges ranking prior to the unsecured loan would be restricted.

2 Floating charge debentures
Debenture stocks can be issued carrying a floating charge. Normally this is a charge on all the present and future assets of a limited company which permits the company, within certain wide limits, to buy and sell assets without recourse to the debenture holders. In normal circumstances, the charge might be considered as floating over the top of assets, but on the happening of certain events specified in the trust deed constituting the stock, the charge crystallises or hardens on the assets of the company, for the time being, and prevents the company from dealing freely with them. In a liquidation, debenture holders are entitled to repayment out of all the assets covered by the floating charge in priority to unsecured non-preferential creditors and shareholders.

3 Fixed charge debentures
Fixed charge debenture stocks are usually secured on the land and buildings and, possibly, plant and machinery of a limited company. In this case, there are usually permanent restrictions on the sales of assets charged.

In a liquidation the debenture holders receive repayment out of the assets charged, in priority to unsecured non-preferential creditors and shareholders. In recent years, against a background of increasing unpopularity of fixed-interest stocks among investors in an inflationary age, it has sometimes suited companies to offer loan stocks which carry either rights of conversion into ordinary shares, or rights to subscribe at a future date.

Short-term loans

Funds from this source may be defined as borrowings repayable within a year. Short-term debt items (current liabilities) are often shown in a balance sheet as a deduction from current assets to give a net figure. But short-term debts are often a large and permanent feature of companies' balance sheets, although of course individual items may be 'turned over' frequently, and many companies make permanent use of their bank credit, although the level of the loan may fluctuate. Expanding companies frequently make increasing use of their bank facilities until they next make an issue of permanent or long-term capital. The overdraft might then be repaid only to be built up again as expansion continues to the stage when another long-term issue is called for.

A company's short-term borrowing may include bank overdrafts, trade bills, and perhaps hire purchase debts, i.e. formal borrowings carrying defined rates of interest. Of much more importance usually is the amount owed to trade creditors, at effective rates of interest which vary, depending upon the settlement terms under which goods are supplied to the company. Credit from this source may be more than counterbalanced by the amount of credit which the company itself extends to its trade debtors. Finally, there are the amounts owing to other categories of creditors, the principal one usually being Government departments (taxes, National Insurance).

Other arrangements

Although they are strictly part of corporate capital and debt the following arrangements reduce the demands for capital and may have a place in the financial strategy:

leasing of plant and equipment,
sale and leaseback of property,
factoring of debts,
hire purchase.

How much capital?

Management varies the finance needed in the business by adding to or reducing its assets. Thus, for example, better control of stocks and debtors reduces the short term funds required to finance them.

Similarly, a decision to sell and lease back a factory or warehouse effects a compensating reduction in the amount of permanent capital required in the business. But let us assume that the company is currently being operated efficiently, with economic 'amounts' of various assets in proportions which the management has decided are best suited to the long-term objectives.

It is the responsibility of the financial management to consider future changes in the capital requirement, and to make plans accordingly. Cash flow projections take into account various cash movements relating to 'capital account' transactions in assets as well as those relating to the trading operation of the company. The projections assess what changes are likely to arise relating to financial requirements and when they are likely to occur. It is desirable to indicate the degree of confidence in the forecasts and their underlying assumptions and in some instances a 'range of possibilities' may be useful.

Armed with this information, the company has a fair idea of its future capital requirements and can proceed to make its financial plan.

Factors affecting choice of finance

The financial plan should be designed to provide the company with adequate finance, taking into account likely variations in requirements, as cheaply as possible, and within acceptable degrees of risk. The selection of sources of finance should be made accordingly.

No company has complete freedom of choice. As regards equity capital, only the quoted public company can approach the public with an issue of shares. Furthermore, there are limits to the amount of long-term loan capital that can be issued by any company. In the case of bank loans stringent tests may be applied to ensure that adequate security is available.

Relative costs

The cost of long-term loan capital is clearly defined in the contractual obligation to pay a stated rate of interest during the period of the loan. The rate of payment on preference capital is also fixed, but as the payment is a distribution by way of dividend it is made out of profits which have borne corporation tax. In the case of a company paying tax at 40% on all its profits a dividend of £60 would 'cost' £100 of pre-tax profits. Corporation tax therefore makes preference capital relatively expensive in relation to other fixed-coupon securities. Preference issues are now infrequent, and many companies have repaid their preference shares by issuing loan stock in exchange. But there have been instances of companies which have reached the limit of their borrowing powers, and which have found it better to increase their borrowing base by issuing further preference rather than ordinary shares.

The current cost of short-term borrowing is also known. The rate of interest on bank loans is clearly stated, and the effective rates of interest on commercial bills, trade credit and hire purchase financing can be fairly easily calculated. These rates, however, may be subject to alteration either immediately or within a comparatively short period. Thus a comparision of the costs of long-term and short-term borrowings over a medium to long period is very much a matter of opinion concerning the future course of interest rates.

The cost of equity capital cannot be ascertained precisely. Indeed, there is sometimes confusion as to how it is to be regarded. This confusion arises from the tendency to make a distinction between the interests of 'the company' and of 'the equity shareholders', whereas to deal adequately with the question of the comparative costs of various types of capital it is essential to regard the company and its shareholders as one. Thus to speak of loan capital 'costing 6% net of tax' is to say that it costs the equity shareholders £6 of their annual profits, net of corporation tax, to borrow £100.

What then is the cost to the shareholder of employing his own money in the business? Obviously it cannot be the dividend payments he receives and which will be paid to him in the future; these are the rewards of his investment, not the cost. His cost is properly regarded as an opportunity cost, the cost of foregoing the return he could obtain by investing in the shares of a company with similar prospects and carrying a similar degree of risk. Trying to quantify this hypothetical return is obviously very much a matter of opinion and judgement. As equity capital bears the highest risk, one would expect it to offer a higher return than any other form of finance. This return will come in the form of annual dividend payments plus any capital gain (or less any loss) in the event of a future sale. As the share price at the time of the sale will itself be largely determined by expectations regarding future dividends at that time, the shareholder's expected return can be said to consist entirely of the stream of all future dividends. The rate of return is that rate of discount which, if applied to all future dividends, would equate their present value to the current cost of the shares. In the case where the dividends increase annually at a fixed rate, the rate of discount is equal to the sum of the current dividend yield plus the rate of growth per year. For practical purposes, therefore, the rate of return on an equity share is often taken as the current dividend yield plus an estimate of the likely growth rate in the next few years. In view of the large element of uncertainty in making the necessary forecasts, there is generally little merit in attempting to be more precise.

The effect of gearing

If a company borrows funds at a fixed rate of interest, and is then able to earn a higher rate of return on these funds, the difference accrues to the equity shareholders. Subsequently, any change in the overall rate of return is magnified at the level of equity earning, and this is commonly referred to as the 'gearing' effect achieved by introducing prior-charge capital.

An example illustrates. Let us assume that Company A has capital employed of £1 million consisting entirely of equity shareholders' funds. Let us also assume that it earns profits at a rate of 15% before tax on this capital, and that profits are taxed at 40%. The position is as follows:

Company A	
Equity shareholders' funds	£1,000,000
Pre-tax profit	£150,000
Less: Tax	£60,000
Earned for equity	£90,000
Earnings rate for equity (net of tax)	9%

Company B has also a total capital employed of £1 million, but £300,000 of it has been raised in the form of a 10% debenture. We have the following position:

Company B	
10% Debenture	£300,000
Equity shareholders' funds	£700,000
Total Capital employed	£1,000,000
Pre-interest profit	£150,000
Less: Debenture interest	£30,000
Taxable profit	£120,000
Less: Tax	£48,000
Earned for equity	£72,000
Earnings rate for equity (net of tax)	10.3% approx

In the latter case an element of 'gearing' has been introduced. This means that any movement in the basic rate of profit earned on the overall capital employed will be magnified at the level of equity earnings, whereas in the case of Company A earnings will move exactly in step with profitability. This is illustrated in figure 3.1.

Company A	*(a)*	*(b)*	*(c)*
Rate of Return	15%	20%	10%
Pre-tax Profit	£150,000	£200,000	£100,000
Less: Tax (40%)	£ 60,000	£ 80,000	£ 40,000
Earned for Equity	£ 90,000	£120,000	£ 60,000
(% change)	–	(+33.3%)	(−33.3%)
Company B	*(a)*	*(b)*	*(c)*
Rate of Return	15%	20%	10%
Pre-tax Profit	£150,000	£200,000	£100,000
Less Debenture Interest	£ 30,000	£ 30,000	£ 30,000
Profit before tax	£120,000	£170,000	£ 70,000
Tax (40%)	£ 48,000	£ 68,000	£ 28,000
Earned for equity	£ 72,000	£102,000	£ 42,000
(% charge)	–	(+41.7%)	(−41.7%)

Figure 3.1 The effect of gearing on equity earnings

The effect of introducing gearing is to improve the rate of growth in equity earnings if the profitability rises, but at the risk of magnifying the fall if profitability declines.

Flexibility

The purpose of the financial plan is to provide the company with adequate, but not excessive, finance and must allow for fluctuations. In practice, this generally means making appropriate use of short-term finance to deal with short-term fluctuations in the demand for funds. This would apply, for example, in a seasonal business where there are wide swings in the level of current assets in the course of a year. However, there are also occasions when a cash flow projection shows a need for funds for, say, a two-year period in which case management will presumably consider the possibility of raising medium-term finance.

Risk

The introduction of prior charges into a company financial structure increases the risk borne by the equity shareholders in two respects. First, there is the increased risk to the ordinary shareholder's income. If the company does badly the decline in profits is emphasised at the level of equity earnings, and dividends may have to be cut. Secondly, if the company does so badly that it has to be liquidated, the prior-charge claimants have to be satisfied in full before any distribution is made to shareholders.

Perhaps even more important is that too much gearing can put the firm in jeopardy. This could be true, for example, of a highly-geared company which operates in an industry subject to wide swings in profitability. In a particularly bad year it may have to default on the interest payments on its loan capital and may be forced into liquidation. A company which is over-dependent on short term credit is at even greater risk; it must ensure that sufficient funds are available by a certain date in the relatively near future. In the extreme case, a company which is making excessive use of credit repayable on demand or at very short notice is particularly vulnerable. It may be pressed for repayment at a time when it is least able to repay, perhaps because its resources have been overstretched due to rapid expansion of the business, stockpiling, new facilities etc.

Choice of capital structure

The foregoing sections have briefly examined the sources of funds available to a company, and have considered the main factors which management takes into account in deciding how to finance its operations. The actual decision reached will depend not only on what financial targets the management has set for the company, but also on its attitude towards the degree of acceptable risk, its views concerning the future of the company's business, and perhaps its views on the future course of interest rates and of inflation. Even when managements are known to have broadly similar objectives, their opinions regarding the ideal corporate financial structure can vary considerably. Indeed, it is quite striking how many leading UK companies have made little or no use of long-term loan capital.

Every company makes some use of the short-term credit. Some of it is interest-free (e.g. taxation due to be paid at a future date), and most companies find it convenient, and probably cheap, to make some use of normal trade credit. In deciding how much more of its needs it will satisfy from short-term sources (e.g. by bank overdraft) the company will first consider the 'profile' of cash requirements in the short-to-medium term, based on the cash flow projection and taking into account the likely margin of error. There is good reason to finance a temporary need from short-term sources. This consideration apart, the proportion of short-term finance in the balance sheet should be decided by balancing its relative cheapness against the risks attached to being dependent on short-term finance.

Current liabilities are often deducted from the total value of assets in a balance sheet to show net capital employed. This amount requires financing on a more permanent basis. The composition of the financing is known as the company's capital structure, the basic question being 'what proportion of our long-term capital should consist of prior-charge capital (i.e. capital ranking before equity capital and, therefore, including both preference and loan capital) bearing a fixed rate of return?'

Prior-charge capital can be obtained at a lower cost than equity funds, and this is particularly true of loan capital. It is probably advantageous for most companies to obtain some of their finance from the prior-charge sources. An upper limit to prior-charge financing is set by the conventional requirements of the investors concerned, e.g. 'yardsticks' concerning cover for loan stocks or the requirement of preference shareholders for assets and income protection for their investment. Against these yardsticks the great majority of UK companies are remarkably 'undergeared'. This may be due to traditional financial conservatism; to pessimism concerning the course of future profits, even in inflated money terms; or failure to appreciate fully the cost advantages of fixed interest stocks. The introduction of corporation tax added emphasis to this last factor, and in recent years more use has been made of this source of finance.

Considerations of risk, from the point of view of the equity shareholder, are also relevant in fixing a prudent limit to the degree of gearing. While there is probably general agreement that in nearly all companies some measure of gearing enhances the prospects of the equity shareholders, it is also true that there is a limit to the amount of prior-charge capital that it would be desirable to introduce. If a company has a 'reasonable' element of gearing, both lenders and equity shareholders are content: the former with the safety of their loan and interest, and the latter that the potential of their investment has been increased without a disproportional increase in risk.

If the degree of gearing is now materially raised, the risk of both parties is increased; the rate of interest on the loan capital might have to be raised, and the risk to the equity element may become unacceptably high. This whole question is very much a matter of opinion and judgement, upon which a company may wish to consult its financial advisers.

Getting a stock exchange quotation

In the discussion so far it has been assumed that the company is able to approach any source of finance it chooses. As a company's demand for funds increases past a certain level, its ability to raise enough capital tends to depend on whether its shares are quoted on a stock exchange. In the case of many small but growing companies, therefore, there comes a stage when the owners and directors have to think seriously about 'getting a quotation'. Other reasons for going public include considerations of personal taxation, of estate duty liabilities, or the owners may simply wish to realise part of the capital invested in their business. From the point of view of the company's finances, the main advantage of a quotation is access to new sources of funds. The company with a quotation can offer new shares, and also finds it easier to obtain loan capital.

Directors thinking of getting a quotation should seek competent professional advice at an early stage. Some firms of stockbrokers have facilities for advising on and sponsoring companies coming to the market for the first time, but for sizeable issues of this kind it is more usual for a merchant bank to give advice on manner and timing, and the leading merchant banks have considerable experience as 'issuing houses'. It is important for the company and its issuing houses to get to know one another and to establish a position of mutual trust well in advance of the approach to a stock exhange.

The issuing house applies its own criteria to determine whether the company is in a position to seek a quotation, and is concerned in the main with the soundness and prospects of the business. Most companies brought to the market are relatively unknown to the investing public, who place a good deal of reliance on the faith and competence of the issuing house. The latter will therefore wish to ensure a sound and attractive investment. Its own reputation as an issuing house is at stake.

Getting a quotation means that thereafter a company will be committed to a public body of investors. The undertaking given to the Stock Exchange obliges the company to issue interim reports, to make a preliminary statement of the year's results as soon as these are known and to give shareholders early information about acquisitions, change of control, capital raising and the like. These statements, the publication of the Annual Report and Chairman's Statement and the proceedings at the annual general meeting are all likely to attract comment from the financial press.

The Unlisted Securities Market (USM)

For some small and growing companies the USM may offer an attractive alternative to a full quotation on the Stock Exchange. Costs and information requirements are less. It is necessary to have an official stockbroker to enter the market and he may also act as a sponsor, or some other body may fill that role.

All this will have the effect, if the standing of the company is good and its management and profitability sound, of promoting its future development and helping, when the time arises, for its capital needs to be fulfilled. However, the market place is a hard taskmaster and there is certainly doubt as to whether a company should seek a quotation for its shares if there is a substantial likelihood of capital hunger and a prospective lowering of profitability. It is considered that in such circumstances it might be better for a company to be sold while it is still privately owned, to someone who wishes to expand in its field of activity and has the resources to take account of its difficulties.

This summary deals overall with the normal methods of capital raising for companies in industry; in summary there is no doubt that, for any company wishing to go forward, the financial plan and the choice of advisers are of the utmost importance.

4 Long-term capacity planning and capability planning

Foster Rogers

The analytical framework

The traditional approach to long-term planning prior to making an investment decision has been to consider such issues as:

historical demand patterns,
factors concerned with economies of scale,
availability of labour,
availability of factory premises.

The information sought, as well as the analytical processes, relied more on the conceptual thinking of Adam Smith and the environment of Scotland in the eighteenth century than the environment of the 1980s with such dimensions as global competition and rapidly changing technologies. For many companies operating in the northern hemisphere, planning takes place within the social framework of the post-industrial society.

This chapter presents an analytical framework providing a series of issues which will have to be considered when making long-term capacity decisions. The relative importance of these items varies, dependent upon the industry and geographical location in which the company operates. While the major thrust of this chapter is concerned with conventional manufacturing industry, in some countries over 60% of the economic activity is in the service sector. The planning for, and the acquisition of, capacity that has taken place in some segments of the service sector is very impressive. The activities of the banking industry in adopting and exploiting the new technologies available have not only allowed the industry to increase efficiency but also to broaden product range. The retail distribution trade in foods and general goods has developed a logistical capability quite equal to anything in Japan. In almost every high street in the United Kingdom there are examples of sophisticated high-technology inventory control, material handling and distribution systems. These organisations have a cost structure which allows them to generate above-average financial returns, enjoy favourable comparisons with equivalent organisations in other parts of the world and, in some cases, exploit a competitive advantage in overseas markets.

The manufacturing environment

One of the first issues to be examined is the competitive environment in which the organisation is operating. An analysis must be undertaken of the competitive advantage or otherwise that each section of the business enjoys. The sections may be separated into groups of products, customers, geographical regions, technologies, manufacturing processes as well as factories.

The aim is to establish the competitive position of each section compared with similar sections in the same or similar industries, together with a comparison between the best in the industry. This analysis enables the organisation to establish the size and nature of the performance gap at the earliest possible stage, since failure to do so may mean an investment in further capacity which will only perpetuate an unfavourable gap.

There are three states to be considered. The first, where the gap is negative, requires further operational analysis to understand the background reasons. Possible reasons could be:

1. the level of technology employed in the manufacturing process,
2. the volume of activity in the particular section as the result of a poor marketing position,
3. a production facility which handles too many products of a too wide variety,
4. the product may not be engineered for manufacture.

The second is where the gap is positive. The issues are much more strategic and suggest a series of questions:

1. Is the competitive advantage in the section defensible against competitors' responses?
2. Is the competitive advantage potentially long-lasting or is it the result of transient actions?
3. Can the advantage be extended to other product groups which do not enjoy this advantage?
4. Is there a fundamental reason for this advantage? Is it the result of superiority in design, engineering, manufacture, or marketing?

The third is where there is no performance gap at the moment. It requires analysis of the momentum of the competitive position of the manufacturing capability.

The result of this gap will enable a framework of strategic decisions to be formulated which represent the basis for the creation of a manufacturing strategy.

Developing a manufacturing strategy

In many organisations, the manufacturing function is seen as the millstone around the corporate neck, incurring costs, always requiring investments, the centre of industrial relations problems, sometimes failing to produce what the marketing function would like to offer the customer. This perception is not helped by the absence of a coherent manufacturing strategy. It is imperative that a consistent and coherent manufacturing strategy be established. The manufacturing function must ensure that the enormous resources are directed so that they can be utilised as a strategic weapon.

The use of these resources must ensure that short-, medium- and long-term manufacturing decisions are all focussed so that the long-term viability of the organisation is guaranteed. This strategy must be established in broad outline so that a proper perspective for investment in long-term capacity can be made. There are two basic manufacturing strategies, reactive and proactive.

Reactive manufacturing strategy

In an organisation with a reactive manufacturing strategy the overall business objectives are paramount. Marketing strategies are devised in a fairly conventional manner based upon considerations of product range, product line pricing, quality levels, delivery and service levels and supporting promotional activities. Manufacturing is perceived as a constraint to satisfy the business objectives of the organisation. The manufacturing function is very reactive to this situation and has historically taken the position, 'Tell us what you want making and we will make sure everybody does their best and we should be able to supply!' Fortunately, in most circumstances the manufacturing function has been able to respond to the needs of the organisation. However, it is usually achieved in an unplanned manner, with achievement of one task accompanied by the subsequent delay of others.

In consequence of this strategy the manufacturing function becomes obsessed with unit costs, productivity issues are concerned with cost reduction, while investments in capacity are protected and in some cases increased. Capacity is the essential ingredient in allowing the function to be reactive!

Proactive manufacturing strategy

In an organisation with a proactive manufacturing strategy the overall commercial business objectives are the same, but the supporting strategies from within are structured in a different manner. The marketing strategies as well as the manufacturing strategies are devised in parallel. The dimensions of the marketing strategies may be similar to those in the reactive case, but they are constructed in conjunction with and taking account of the constraints and opportunities of the total operations strategy. The dimensions of the operations strategy include:

1 total unit cost of the product,
2 total lead times of manufacture including procurement lead time,
3 the reliability of the product and the process in terms of quality and delivery,
4 batch sizes and sequencing of work.

These dimensions will be determined from a strategy which addresses these questions:

- What will be made in the existing capacity?
- What products will be procured from outside the organisation?
- What processes will be used in making what products?

In answering these questions two sets of priorities will emerge, one set concerned with the structural nature of the manufacturing facility, the other with the infrastructure of the manufacturing function.

Facility decisions

Facility decisions are concerned with:

1 The total amount of manufacturing and logistics capacity provided for each product line in each segment.
2 How this capacity is allocated into operating units (factories, warehouses), their size and structure (a few large plants or many small units), their location, and the degree of their specialisation (product or process orientation).
3 The type of manufacturing equipment and production process to be used in each of the factories.
4 The span of production process. This is the extent of vertical integration intended, which implies the amount of supplier involvement. (Are all the inputs to be purchased so that the process is only one of assembly?). The balance between different capacities for separate operations may be such that the use of specialist subcontractors may be needed.

Infrastructure decisions

Infrastructure decisions are concerned with:

1 Policies that determine and control the loading of work into the factories and their implications for raw material purchasing, finished goods inventory and distribution.

2 Policies that control the movement of goods through the factories. This includes consideration of product and process design, labour relations involving shift patterns and multimanning of machines, production scheduling, quality control, and work-in-process inventory control.
3 The organisation of the manufacturing functions so that all these decisions can be made and provide the stimulus for them to be implemented.

These decisions all are interdependent. The annual total effective capacity of a factory depends on whether the production rate is to be kept at a constant rate over the year (facility decision) or alternatively is to be subject to many schedule changes in an attempt to match the vagaries of demand (infrastructure decision). Similarly, labour force policies will be influenced by location and process choices, which in turn interact with the decisions on vertical integration. The competitiveness of the suppliers could have considerable impact on purchasing policy which directly influences the long-term capacity planning issue.

These decisions can only be structured in a meaningful manner if they are judged against the competitive performance gap analysis described in an earlier section. Whatever the competitive circumstances of the organisation, there must be coherence in the manufacturing strategy that emerges from the foregoing analysis. Skinner (1974) has argued that one way of achieving this coherence is to divide the total manufacturing task into a series of focussed units each responsible for a limited series of activities and objectives:

> 'Each (manufacturing unit should have) its own faciities in which it can concentrate on its particular manufacturing task, using its own workforce, management approaches, production control, organisational structure, and so forth. Quality and volume levels are not mixed; worker training and incentives have a clear focus; and engineering of processes, equipment, and materials handling are specialised as needed. Each (unit) gains experience rapidly by focussing and concentrating every element of its work on those limited essential objectives which constitute its manufacturing task'.

To take advantage of this concept of the focused factory, manufacturing organisations must be able to manage the resultant diversity of units and tasks. In an organisation having a proactive strategy, the individual units will be very responsive and flexible to the requirements of the marketing function and thus enable the overall business objective to be achieved. However, the manufacturing management responsibility of organising such a function is very different. Each individual unit has its own clearly-defined task, perhaps a different series of functional objectives as well as putting a unique set of demands upon the manufacturing infrastructure. Some units might have a product focus while others have a process focus. The implications of this divergence of focus are significant. The product focus units could have subordinate linkages with the marketing function whilst the process focus units may have a dominant linkage with marketing but perhaps a subordinate linkage with the technology function of the organisation as well as other product-focused units.

Developing a strategy for automation

The analysis needed to establish a manufacturing strategy has now been completed. This should result in a series of identifiable focused units, each having its own competitive position.

The implementation process must now be considered. Only if this process is successful will a competitive advantage be achieved and sustained. Automation of the manufacturing process must be considered. While there are opportunties for automated factories and factories of the future to be installed on green field sites, the majority of structural changes will take place in existing manufacturing facilities.

There are two approaches to automation in manufacturing: one creates dedicated production or process lines for each unit; the other a flexible automated system. The dedicated line is designed to operate with low product variability and high demand with low fluctuation. Any variations in demand are accommodated by changes in the level of product inventory. It has the advantage of potential low unit costs and predictable infrastructure costs, but suffers from exposure to fundamental demand shifts. However, providing this exposure is recognized and understood by corporate management, it presents the most effective investment in capacity that can be made. There are examples in the component sector of the automotive industry of dedicated production lines being created from existing machine tools together with purpose designed and engineered transfer equipment. This has achieved significant unit cost reduction with modest investment. The resultant increase in effective capacity has been quite high, but achievement of this increase may require changes in labour shift patterns.

The flexible automated system has been designed to cope with high product variability as well as high fluctuations in demand. The potential benefits of such a system are considerable, but it is usually limited in scope of operations. The concept that one batch of a thousand would have the same manufacturing cost in the system as a thousand batches of one-off is very appealing. These systems are described as flexible manufacturing systems and many have been installed all over the world. While it is true that they can manufacture small batches of a family of similar parts at substantially the same cost as a larger batch, the capacity created has been too large for the market to absorb.

However, substantial gains have been made by some companies who have taken the opportunity to make facility-type decisions to engineer their product for both marketing and manufacture. While the flexible systems have great potential, there are constraints which need to be overcome. One of the major obstacles is that designers have worked within the reactive manufacturing system. This has led to a plethora of manufacturing methods and a large variety of similar engineering details. The consideration of automated manufacturing units has persuaded design, production engineering, marketing and manufacture to examine the areas for standardisation while still maintaining design freedom. A medium-sized precision engineering company operating in the UK has been able to reduce the number of uniquely shaped metal cutting tools from 2000 to 146 in a period of less than one year. This reduction was achieved in preparation for the installation of a flexible manufacturing system. The benefits gained were not only in direct operating costs but also in infrastructure costs.

Each product or process-focused unit should have its own strategy. In some instances the new high technology and automated dedicated production line will replace the existing capacity. In other cases creative solutions may be found, by using existing equipment with high technology transfer equipment. The robot represents, at a simple level, a means of linking existing machines into a manufacturing system. The majority of robots installed in manufacturing systems so far have been in the automobile industry, but an increasing number are finding their way into other industries. The potential robot utilisation during the next ten years, even at a substitution rate of four people to one robot, will not increase the total unemployment figure significantly, especially if the new jobs created are taken into consideration. In addition, the resulting increase in productivity should yield an improvement in the market position of the company, producing additional sales volume and even further employment. This has proved to be the case in the Japanese manufacturing industry. The opportunity for using robots in existing plants is very exciting. Providing a dynamic and flexible manufacturing organisation has been created these opportunities can be realised.

Planning human resources

Both the approaches to automated manufacture outlined inevitably require less direct labour, although the demand for supporting staff will increase. The need to invest in training for new skills such as maintenance technicians and computer programmers is an important factor in capacity planning.

A recent survey published by the Institute of Policy Studies estimated that over the period 1981-1983 there was a net loss of 34,000 jobs associated with the use of microelectronics in British manufacturing industry – about 5% of the overall reduction in manufacturing employment over that period.

Research by Aston University suggests that the introduction of CNC machines is associated with a net job loss of 2-3 per machine. In the same study, it was estimated that 2-5 jobs were lost per active robot and from this they deducted that 1,500-3,500 jobs may have been lost in 1983, whereas it is estimated that at least 1,500 new jobs have been created in the same period in maintenance and computer programming associated with these machines.

Automated manufacture represents an opportunity for the UK manufacturing industry to regain its competitive advantage. However, investments in automated manufacture should achieve more than a unit cost reduction, they should also be an essential part of the corporate strategy of the organisation. It is inevitable that labour policies will have to be changed, but these are a necessary prerequisite to regaining competitive advantage.

Planning for competitive advantage

In the post-industrial society of the majority of developed countries, manufacturing still represents an important wealth-generating sector of economy. For each economy, depending so much on a successful manufacturing industry which must compete globally with developed and developing countries, long-term capacity planning in automation is a precursor to achieving the efficiency needed for economic success.

The Advisory Council on Applied Research and Development (AARD 1983) gave its views on the value of automation in manufacturing arguing that:

> 'A competitive product requires design for manufacture (manufacture in this context means the totality of the process that has come to be termed 'Group Technology').
>
> A competitive edge requires the best manufacturing technology.'

These two simple statements provide a framework for the consideration of long-term capacity planning and capability planning:

1. Manufacturing technology is a corporate management responsibility and the main board must monitor its appropriate implementation.
2. Corporate strategy must be coherent with the strategies of marketing, operations and finance.
3. Investment decisions in advanced manufacturing technology have to take account of facility and infrastructure savings as well as intangible benefits, together with the consequences of not investing.
4. The implementation of advanced manufacturing techniques should take into account the eventual integration into a total system. The achievement

of this objective requires detailed planning and the provision of trained people at all levels of the organisation.

Long-term capacity planning and capability planning require all managements to take a strategic view of their competitive position in the world's market place. This strategic view is only arrived at by detailed analysis of the products, processes and markets in which the organisation is currently competing, together with those that show profit potential in the future. Any further capacity decision should be aimed at achieving a competitive advantage which can be exploited to guarantee long-term success for the organisation.

5 The history, culture and leadership of a company

John Fawn

Why leadership is important

If two companies compete in the same market, with identical facilities and finance-raising capability, one company will be more successful than the other The reason is a combination of the history, culture and leadership of the two companies. Any planning which takes place without recognising what has happened in the past and what is acceptable as a course of action, is valueless.

All companies are evaluated in the market place, by customers, bank managers, suppliers and competitors, on the basis of their previous track record. A bank manager, for instance, is very wary when lending to a newly-established business venture, simply because the company has yet to establish itself as successful. If he is to lend money he will want to convince himself that business acumen exists within the company, however excellent the product might be. In the eyes of a bank manager, the best business to lend to is the one that has experienced a continuous history of success. Suppliers look for continuity of business and a long-term ability to pay for the goods supplied when doing business. Customers look for a tradition of quality of goods and service when buying as well as price and a product that does the required job.

Why should a successful history be any indicator of what might happen in the future? When an entrepreneur founds a business, he also sets the norms and values which are used by that company. If these norms and values do not produce a coherent business, the business is likely to fail. If the business is run coherently, and success follows, the success reinforces the existing norms and values. A winning formula is always worth maintaining.

The creation of this winning formula is the responsibility of the leader of the company. In small newly-created companies, he is often the entrepreneur that founded the company, but this is not always the case. In many companies, not all the skills needed to run the company are found in one man and a true partnership exists. When the Rolls-Royce company was founded early in the century, tradition looks back on the Hon. C.S. Rolls and Henry Royce as creating the company. In practice, Rolls had a comparatively small role, and the company was really created by the engineering and production skills of Henry Royce, the general management and marketing flair of Claude Johnson, and the financial astuteness of accountant Clairmont. Royce, Johnson and Clairmont developed a company that in less than five years created a product with a reputation for excellence. Since that time the description 'Rolls-Royce' has been synonymous with the best.

Leaders can also emerge part way through the life of a company and change its established direction and value system. Robert Townsend transformed a poorly performing car rental company called Avis into a force to challenge the market leaders Hertz. He did this primarily by his leadership style which delegated decision taking to a level where managers were forced to manage and by revitalising the corporate image through the now famous 'We Try Harder' advertising campaign. On the other hand, John Egan revitalised the fortunes of Jaguar Cars in the early 1980's by returning to much of the value system of Jaguar's founder, Sir William Lyons. This came about after a period in the late 1970s when the then British Leyland Group had tried to establish a corporate identity which was alien to a specialist car manufacturer.

What is interesting when looking at creators of norms and culture is that they are often innovators who were prepared to evolve the company in line with the needs of the world. However, they set certain standards which are inviolable, and often present a contradictory mixture of being great innovators with inflexible rules. When these men are finally replaced, the culture they leave behind is so strong that the company continues as if they were still there. If the system is perceived to allow flexibility within these standards the company can continue to thrive. There is however a danger that the company will cease to meet the needs of a changing market place.

When a new man is appointed chief executive or managing director, he has to establish the style with which he wishes to operate. A man whose career has developed within that company is likely to have reached the top position by conforming to the established norms and values. It is highly likely that such an appointee, if he comes from within the company, will wish to continue the existing system. When in turn he comes to retire, it is likely that the man that takes his place will again be in the same mould. It is in this way that companies build up traditions of being run by engineers, accountants or marketeers. At IBM it is almost inconceivable that the top man could have got there without having come through the marketing organisation at some stage in his career.

A new chief executive who has been appointed from outside the company is almost certainly going to cause culture shock to the system. He is likely to know or subscribe to few of the norms that his fellow directors on the board hold dear. The options are for him to learn and accept the accepted values or for the organisation to change its patterns. In practice, a little of both happens, but this takes time. A company which has had an autocratic leader finds it difficult to adapt to a new chief executive who has a style which is participative. The board members are simply not used to taking participative initiatives which would have been unacceptable in the days of the autocratic leader. It may well be that nationalised industries, especially those which have been subjected to a succession of politically appointed highly talented outsiders, have suffered considerably from having to change their value systems with each change of leader.

The leadership of the company is so important that planning must be done in close collaboration. The most effective corporate planning organisations often report directly to the managing director and ignore his objectives at their peril.

Creating a culture

The leader figure within the company creates the culture and value system. What are the factors which can lead to the setting of the value system?

The first factor involves geography and national heritage. National resources, proximity to reliable markets and ease of alternative sources of income must set standards for individual people.

In the formative years of the United States of America, the availability of land was one of the main attractions to immigrants. Skilled people in Europe found the opportunities available in the USA less attractive than did the less skilled farm labourers. When the United States needed the tools that skilled men in Europe provided, they had to be produced by people without the skill. The only way to do this was through splitting the process into simple operations which non-skilled people could do. Thus the modern industrial process was developed and gained acceptance. The same sort of process had also been developed in England by Marc Isambard Brunel (father of the great Isambard Kingdom Brunel) at Portsmouth dockyard for the manufacuture of wooden block and tackle equipment, but the different social pressures prevented its adaptation to more general use in England. The industrial culture and value system that developed in the United States has to this day maintained that country in the forefront of industrialised nations. Europe on the other hand has struggled on with its legacy of skilled but inflexible tradesmen which is only now being challenged. Japan by contrast, has a tradition of isolation and self-sufficiency based on its location and geography. The map of Japan shows mountainous islands where major habitation is only possible along the costal plains and communication and travel is difficult. The size of the population has put usable land at a premium. Companies have developed with an emphasis on saving space and having local supply networks. The

Kanban (Just In Time) type systems which evolved, concentrating on small batch sizes, short lead time, minimal stock levels and close supplier relationships, have made a virtue of these constraints and have given the Japanese a highly competitive management system in a world that demands fast reaction to technology.

At a competitive level Porter (1980) identifies three possible generic strategies:

Cost Leadership
Differentiation
Focus

He observes that it is very difficult for a company to follow two different generic strategies at the same time. Much of this relates to the culture of a company. Referring back to the example of the early Rolls-Royce motorcar, history indicates that the main contribution that the Hon. Charles Rolls made was in defining the market for an up-market differentiated product which was exclusive and reliable. Up to that time Henry Royce had designed a series of two, three and four cylinder motorcars which were similar to other cars, but because of engineering excellence were highly reliable. After the meeting of Rolls and Royce a new company was formed which set about producing a series of up-market motorcars which included the straight six cylinder Silver Cloud and a vee-eight landaulette. It was Claude Johnson who evolved the strategy of concentration on the single model policy of the Silver Ghost. From that time on the company concentrated on producing cars to a very high quality yet ignoring the latest technical innovations until they were proven.

This policy brought with it consequences for the workforce. The design and development engineers were set exacting standards for design and product development. The production workforce was also set standards for craftsmanship which certainly well exceeded those acceptable in the mass production car factories of the day. Indeed there are several stories of Royce returning from his retirement home, first on the south coast of England and then from the south of France and sacking large numbers of the workforce because they were working to less than his increasingly exacting standard. Needless to say these highly skilled men, who were vital to the success of the company, were always taken back the next day when Royce returned home. Finally, standards of worldwide service were set so as to maintain the reputation of the motorcar. Major failures such as broken crankshafts were replaced free of charge simply because Rolls-Royce crankshafts did not fail.

The gross margins required to maintain such an operation (they exceeded 100% in 1907) were large especially when added to the large promotional activity. The prices that had to be charged for such standards could only be obtained at the upper end of the market.

Any attempt by Rolls-Royce at that time to get into the mass motorcar market would have forced the company to reduce its standards or reduce its costs. This would in turn have meant retraining its workforce to accept the lower standards and would certainly have led to a change in the service policy. The changes would have led to a reduction in the exclusivity of the up-market product with a consequential fall in sales. It is highly unlikely that any amount of retraining of the workforce to a new culture would have reduced costs fast enough to compete in the mass market, and the company would almost certainly have failed.

The Jaguar cars experience of the 1970s demonstrates this scenario. Jaguar had become part of the then ailing British Leyland group and, despite being an up-market specialist car manufacturer, was 'absorbed' into the group. The standards expected of the workforce and suppliers were set as that required for the mass car market. The reliability of the product suffered and the Jaguar market declined. The pride of the workforce in producing a special product all but disappeared and morale suffered. When John Egan became managing director his leadership style was in line with the original culture of Jaguar; as a schoolboy in Coventry he must have been aware of the culture. He had to prune the workforce severely to improve productivity to acceptable levels and take the supply network to task for sub-standard quality. Despite all these problems, he was able to build on what remained of the pride in the original company, and re-establish the reputation of the company in the early 1980s.

It follows that the corporate planners should generate proposals which are consistent with the culture of the organisation, in addition to meeting the objectives of the leadership. Where the two are in conflict, the problems must be resolved or action taken to modify either the culture or the leadership objectives.

When you should change your culture

So far I have discussed the importance of leadership, culture and history. Nothing can change the history of a company, but there are times when leadership styles and the culture of organisations do need to be changed.

As the company evolves through the product life cycle differing external influences affect its operation. Ansoff (1984) identifies how the needs change throughout the phases of the life cycle (see figure 5.1).

Demand Stage	Critical function
Evolutionary	General management, research & development
Early growth	Production
Late growth	Marketing
Maturity	General Management, (Research & Development)
Decline	General management

Figure 5.1 Functional needs in the product life cycle

The leadership style of the entrepreneurial product champion in the formative growth phase must in time give way to the need to concentrate on production in early growth and then to the needs of marketing during the late growth phase. As product maturity and then decline sets in, general management skills are required of the leadership. The leadership style must therefore continuously evolve through the product life cycle and this will automatically lead to a gradually altering culture.

Peters and Waterman (1983) suggest that keeping to the business one knows well is one of the major factors which identifies successful companies, together with leadership, culture and an open management style.

The problem arises when the product and its attendant technology become obsolete. An example is the business of electronic signal amplification. The original technology was the thermionic valve, superseded by the transistor which was in turn superseded by the integrated circuit. The market leaders in one technology had developed culture around their techology and failed to adapt to the new technology. It is very rare to find a market leader of one technology becoming the market leader with the replacement technology. One of the reasons is that an established culture simply cannot be changed fast enough to react to a step change in the market place.

Much of the problem revolves around whether to bring in new, often young, people who are conversant with the emergent technology, or whether to retrain older people away from the concepts they are used to. Retraining may not be totally successful, and takes time which may not be available. Displacing people with old technology skills generates the social problem of making people redundant. Mixing the two creates problems by challenging the established hierarchy and culture. In microcomputers, the marketing in parallel of different stages of technology creates the problem of inhibiting the development of a culture. It is difficult for any but the largest suppliers of software to stay in the game when the business environment tends to keep changing at such a rapid pace.

The traditional solution to the problem of obsolete technology is for a large corporation to go out and buy a new company with the emergent technology.

The widespread failure of attempts to integrate them into the old company culture is well documented. Corporations seem to be much more successful if they milk the old company and run it down, while building up the new technology separately. The best course may even be to just run the old business down while squeezing the most profit from the existing product, and then get out of that part of the business.

Perhaps the most difficult task facing the planner is at the end of the product life cycle when a major cultural change may be necessary. It may well be possible by good planning, great leadership and persistence to radically change the culture of a company, thus allowing it to face the challenge of new technology, which can provide complete replacements for the current product base. There are insufficient well documented cases of successful implementations of such a strategy to know whether this is really possible.

The planner and company culture

Much of what the true corporate planner does is to implant ideas of what might be possible in peoples' minds. Long term strategies are often created by planners, but are never implemented by them. The glory of a successful strategy always goes to the functional staff who do the implementation. Planners only get recognised if the strategies go wrong.

Perhaps the most frustrating part of the planner's job is the fact that he works at least two years in advance of things happening. His role is to ensure the ongoing success of the company or corporation by gradually ensuring the evolution of the company culture. He must anticipate the cultural evolutionary situations he has previously worked to create and build on them.

If the planner gets it wrong and the company is asked to change less than the market requires, the company may not be able to react to the new realities of the market place. If he asks the company to change more quickly than the company culture allows then his plans will not fit within the tramlines of acceptable company culture and his ideas will be rejected. Getting it wrong in either direction will put the company at a competitive disadvantage.

The corporate planner must know in a very detailed way how the culture of the company operates. He must be able to anticipate the objectives of the chief executive. He must be able to stand back and take a totally objective view of where the company strategy is leading, and be prepared to challenge both culture and leader if he thinks this is necessary.

6 How to organise planning

John Pittaway and Gerald Owen

Introduction

Business planning involves two main formalised exercises. One is a strategic plan, which looks ahead annually (or less frequently) to define the broad scheme or strategy for a business, phrased in terms of goals and of how they are broadly to be achieved. The other is an annual budget, which is concerned with the immediate tactics needed to achieve the strategy. The budget also monitors whether the strategy is on course, and, if it is not, points to what needs doing to correct matters. The plan and budget taken together constitute a formalised system for an organisation to adapt to change and, if effectively pursued, can be the key to its successful evolution.

This chapter describes how a business planning system may be operated, in medium-sized and larger companies, with particular emphasis on the elements of the strategic planning process.

Reporting structure in a group

Medium-sized and large businesses, particularly those engaged in a range of distinct, major, activities, are often organised as shown in Figure 6.1.

This structure requires rather intricate systems of information processing for effective strategic planning. Occasional reference will be made to simpler systems in less complex organisations.

The organisation is referred to as a group and each major activity is termed a division. The lowest tier businesses are called strategic business units (SBUs). Each SBU has a chief executive who reports directly to the chief executive of the next higher tier, and so on up. Each maintains a full operational and financial reporting system, a prerequisite of effective business planning and control.

SBUs are units in which the group has a controlling interest. They need not be legal entities, because their distinguishing features are business activity, geographical location, or both.

The term 'group chief executive' is used to denote the ultimate authority, in the day-to-day executive management of the group. It can relate to one person or an executive committee. In this kind of complex organisation, the objectives

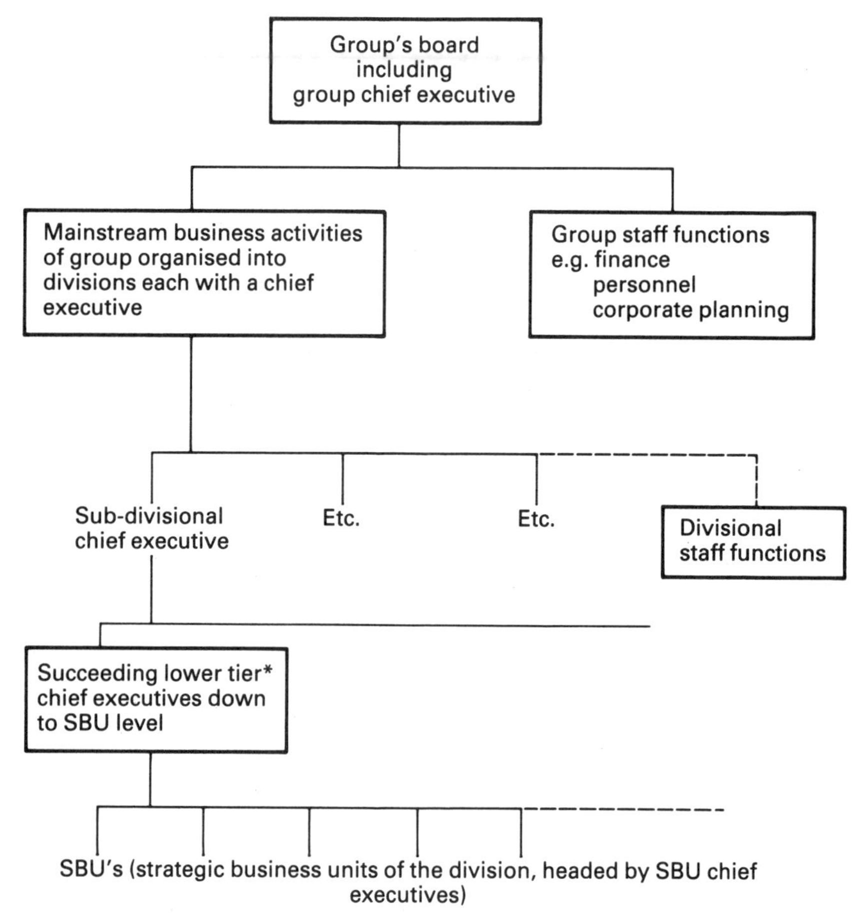

Figure 6.1 Organisation structure of a group

of planning must be to seek the optimal strategy of the group. This involves reconciling the two planning processes termed top-down (which encapsulates the groups's preference for the type of organisation it wishes to be and the objectives it wishes to pursue) and bottom-up (which consolidates the strategies of the various sub-units). There is usually conflict between the two processes which is both desirable and stimulating. For example, the bottom-up approach may be excessively demanding on group financial resources, or conversely, insufficiently growth orientated. Furthermore, an individual business unit may see its future development in activities in which the group may not wish to invest, raising the question of whether the group or the unit's strategy should be modified or the unit divested. Interactions of this kind are the essence of strategic planning and appropriate decisions can only be made following ordered dialogue and an effective two-way flow of information.

It is assumed in this chapter that the strategic plan and the budget are separate exercises. The former is administered by the planning function and the latter by the finance function. Further, the corporate planning function is assumed to possess skills in three main areas: economic and market analysis, technology appraisal and financial analysis. Each professional planner, whatever his main discipline, must be capable of breadth of view and contribute to broad business analysis evaluations.

Information needed for planning

Strategy is concerned with goals and ways of achieving them. The goals are the prime and paramount objectives of the organisation until they have been clearly demonstrated to be not achievable or no longer relevant. In setting objectives a business must understand the strategic situation of its constituent operating units, in current and predicted economic circumstances. This means relating the performance of the activities of each business to those of strategically similar businesses and to direct competitors. 'Strategically similar' means having activities with fundamental characteristics in common. As an example, businesses engaged in basic petrochemicals production and those in steel making are strategically similar in a global sense. They characteristically have low market growths, a preponderance of mature products, high turnover per employee, high capital employed relative to value added, low value added relative to turnover, and low research and development expenditure relative to turnover. Not surprisingly, another common characteristic is below-average return on capital employed. However, some steel makers and basic petrochemical producers have much better returns than others because they are more efficient in some way or another. A more familiar example is non-competing high street retail chains, such as chemists, stationers and some DIY chains which trade at similar levels of value per customer purchase but have very different product ranges.

The planning process requires information about the performance a business can be expected to achieve, having regard to its current strategic characteristics and those planned for the future, and how they will attain those performances. Though many performance measures are financial (e.g. lower product costs, higher turnover of working capital) other equally important measures are non-financial, e.g. market share and product quality ratings.

Other indicators are largely unquantified, notably those to do with human relationships and motivations: these are not within the scope of this chapter but they are important in the dialogues which will be described.

Gathering, assimilating and analysing information is the very substance of the whole strategic process of learning and adaptation. Management must, for the sake of its very survival, at least keep abreast with, and preferably anticipate developments in the external economic and social environment. One of the main responsibilities delegated to strategic planning staff is identifying and analysing all aspects of the environment important to the organisation.

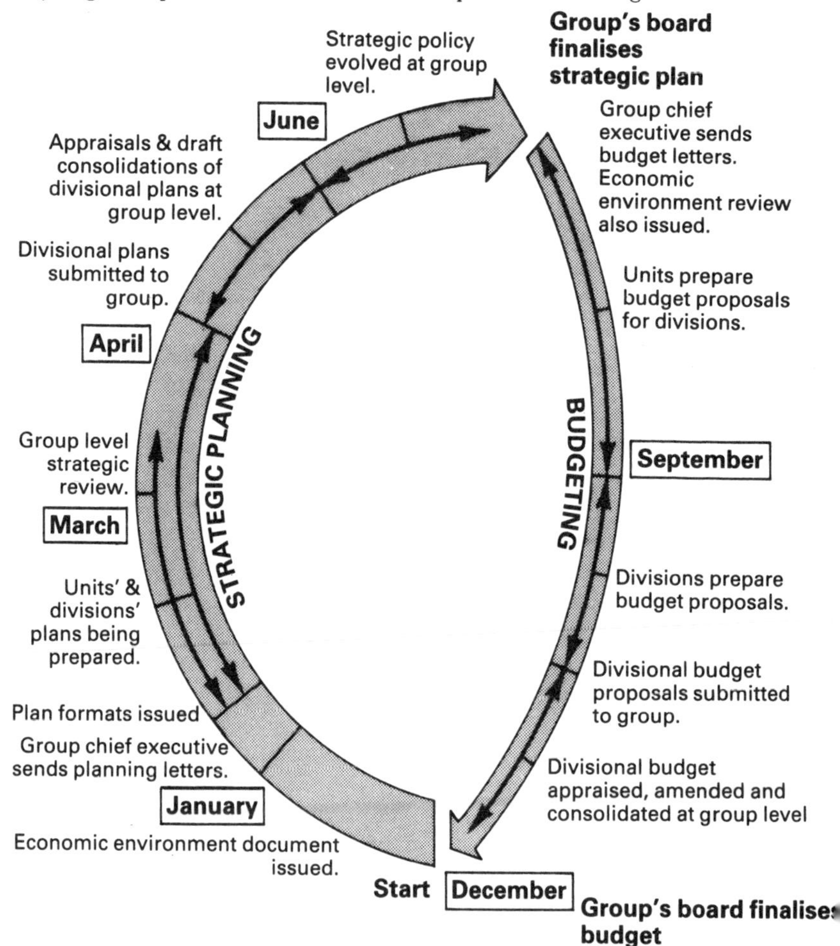

Figure 6.2 Key events and activities in the annual planning cycle

The planning cycle

A planning system can follow an annual cycle from strategic plan to budget, and the process now described (see figure 6.2) is illustrated by breaking into the cycle at the end of the annual budget setting. This is typically December in the case of an organisation whose financial year is January to December, and such phasing of the whole process seeks to avoid intensive sequential (or even simultaneous) annual inquisition on both the strategy and the budget.

An effective planning procedure encompasses a great many individual exercises which are frequently interactive so it cannot be described as a sequence of discrete steps. In particular no distinction can be drawn between a description of the system and a description of how it works. After looking at the planning cycle in terms of budgeting and planning, activities needed to make the whole process work are discussed. The essence of the system is the effective use of information leading to decisions arrived at after much searching argument. The decisions can rarely be amiable agreements between all constituents of the organisation and the dialogues in planning must be disciplined. The purpose of the planning cycle is to decide or confirm objectives; to produce strategies and the tactics within strategies which are all the concern of budgets.

Reviewing and updating strategy

The budgeting process has a framework of strategic bounds or constraints, which has to be re-appraised when the strategy is reviewed and updated. The smaller business, whether independent or part of the group, often lacks the resources needed for frequent examination of its strategic position and while doing all it can in this respect (for example by commissioning selected studies), must make up for its limited resources by enhanced agility and entrepreneurial flair. The smaller unit has shorter chains of command and its chief executive should be involved with the details of all functions of his business and its market environment. Thus one comes nearer to the truly entrepreneurial situation and such units, when operating within large groups, need to be handled with special care.

Even at divisional level a full re-appraisal every year can be an excessive burden. In cases where it is evident there is no significant deviation from the correct strategic course, there is no justification in imposing this burden every year. An abbreviated strategic update may be sufficient, but re-appraising all its strategic axioms at two or three yearly intervals. Ideally, half the division should prepare a full plan and half a brief roll-over plan every year, so balancing the work load upon the group's top management and its corporate planning staff and allowing detailed attention to be focussed on a few businesses. This routine switches the focus of attention from year to year. It also helps to avoid the danger of executives at all levels beginning to regard strategic planning as a ritual, involving no more than a regular refurbishment of earlier arguments. Perhaps the most important general rule in strategic planning is to avoid assuming that past experience will continue.

The planning horizon

The strategic planning horizon of an SBU (the number of years ahead for which it or any of its subsidiary business units should endeavour to plan) is dictated by the nature of its activity. For example, it may not be very meaningful for a business which has to react quickly to current fashions or tastes to try to look further than two years. On the other hand, the group itself must usually look five years ahead given greater diversity in its constituent businesses, because that time span encompasses the lengths of economic cycles which seem to prevail globally as well as nationally. That being so, even businesses with short planning horizons have to produce five year projections as realistically as they can, resorting to every possible analytic technique, even though the third to fifth years might have to be stated solely in financial terms.

Some businesses should endeavour to look ahead for longer periods, e.g. those in steel production, certain chemical plants, development of offshore oil fields, pharmaceuticals and public utility undertakings like electricity supply. Businesses with important longer-term commitments which cannot be assigned without a severe penalty also fall into this category. Examples of the latter have abounded in recent years, notably in shipping and civil aviation. In these cases the planning horizon is determined by the time span of the governing activities. For instance, offshore oil exploration should really have a strategic framework extending at least fifteen years into the future, because it has a gestation period (award of exploration rights to start of commercial production) and discounted payback period of around ten years, and large-scale investment.

The strategy review and update is broad brush compared with the budget exercise. This poses special problems at group and divisional levels. Objectives and strategies need to be developed in an imaginative manner; at the same time they may be constrained by limitations of financial, and sometimes managerial, resources. Divisions need to compete for these resources, but are unable to define or identify precisely some of their investment proposals. Some proposals may be no more precise than 'an acquisition in France or Germany of a packaging machinery manufacturer for £10-20m in year 3 or 4 of the plan'. Problems of this kind have to be made tractable and a system devised to avoid divisions over-bidding for available resources. This entails a well-defined sequence in the interval between finalising the group's budget in December and the update of the group's strategic plan in mid-year. Salient steps in this sequence of work are now outlined briefly, centering upon information for strategic decision and control. Three major actions initiate the process which is shown schematically in figure 6.2.

The 'economic environment' document

First, a document is issued during January describing the environmental assumptions governing all strategic evaluations. This 'economic environment document' is prepared by the corporate planning function and spells out a base scenario of the most likely course of events, against which all the plans (i.e. the SBUs and higher tiers' strategic reviews and updates) have to be prepared. It is quite usual nowadays to plan against more than one scenario. It is recommended to spell out at least one alternative and, for the sake of clarity and brevity, to focus only upon the differences between alternative and base scenario. If just one alternative is used, it usually describes a more adverse environment and is of lower probability than the base. Divisions generally do not plan in detail against this alternative scenario but consider its impact on future profitability and investment decisions. Likewise, at group level the implications of the alternative scenario are considered in relation to future profitability and resource availability. The objective of the analysis is to indicate the risks entailed in pursuing a business strategy reflecting only the base scenario, and thereby devising plans which endeavour to avoid the greatest risks associated with either. Though sometimes more than two scenarios are considered it is doubtful that the resultant range of possible outcomes is of practical value.

Another way of going about things is to examine how a postulated strategy would fare using the most favourable set of circumstances at one extreme, and the least favourable at the other. The objective is to derive a strategy sustainable under all foreseeable external conditions. This approach has been called 'tramline', for obvious reasons. By definition it entails more wide-ranging analysis than that outlined above: so although it is a useful, workable approach for an individual SBU the convolutions involved render it intractable as SBUs are aggregated. It is almost inevitable that the proliferations resulting from its application are unmanageable for a group. The problem is not a matter of computational ability, but of interpretation, i.e. of comparison between the many combinations of strategies and their alternative outcomes. The economic environment document should give an appraisal of the anticipated developments, under the base scenario, in the economies of all parts of the world where the group is likely to operate. Individual argued views should be given in most detail about the countries which have greatest impact on the group's future. These points are most often concerned with assessments of political and economic risks. These considered views should assess economic growth, inflation and currency exchange rates, as well as energy costs (usually in terms of oil price) and the costs of other inputs, like employment and raw materials. The salient risks entailed, if the alternative scenario were to prevail, should also be assessed.

The period covered should be at least five years, beginning with the first year of the new plan, i.e. from the beginning of the following January (eleven months away). Trends expressed as averages per year over the planning period or the economic cycle may be built into the individual country forecasts. Where more than five years perspective is required, it will be concerned with broad aspects such as world economic growth rates, the rise or decline of nations in economic importance and stability, or long term trends in, say, commodity prices.

In smaller companies, the international aspect is often less significant and, in the absence of in-house staff to provide economic scenarios, consultants may be used or a view derived from published forecasts.

The group chief executive's guidance to divisions

Secondly, the group chief executive should send an individual letter to each divisional chief executive to guide him in preparing his strategic plan. He will write under the perspective of the economic environment document, the Group's provisional results and the recently completed budget for the current year. He will highlight major strategic issues which require attention in the divisional strategic plan and indicate whether a detailed or roll-over strategy needs to be produced.

His letters should indicate the allocation and phasing of financial resources for each division over the next few years. These resources are of two kinds: the funds available for the tactical sustenance of existing core businesses, termed core capital expenditure and those available for major strategic moves, termed strategic expenditure. If funds are lacking in either respect he will indicate broadly what should be done about the situation, which might include selling assets. These indications are expressed in very broad terms at this stage in the planning cycle, e.g. whether significantly more or less is likely to be available for strategic expenditure than had been anticipated in the previous year's plan. Generally, unless a business is patently in irreversible decline, core capital expenditure is not a major question. The amounts required to sustain core businesses will be apparent by considering replacement needs, the natural growth of the business and efficiency improvement investments. Assigning even a tentative figure for strategic expenditure is a different matter, although funds availability may well set an overall limit. Such an assessment is made from a broad brush estimate of the performance and requirements of the core businesses over the coming 5 years, based on the previous 5 year strategic plan, the latest budget and economic environment forecasts.

There are no hard and fast rules to differentiate core capital expenditure from strategic expenditure: it all depends upon the nature of the business. Adding a new factory to a business as part of an expansionary thrust could well constitute strategic expenditure. Equivalent capacity added to existing factories to exploit anticipated normal market growth would probably be core capital expenditure. All acquisitions as well as investments in developing companies would be seen as strategic investments.

The indications about possible strategic and core capital allocations are a first approximation to what will eventually be included in the group plan, to be finalised in July. Progress to the final allocation is achieved by successive trial iterations, each with the aim of achieving a better approximation to the desired end result. This entails the sort of interactive dialogue, already mentioned and described more fully below, to bring about the flow of information with inbuilt feedback; this interaction gives more precision to the group's allocation decisions in mid-year.

All other exercises in the February to July plan preparation are analogous to this capital allocation example. They involve identifying the key themes in the divisional and lower tier strategies which, taken together, will be major determinants of the group plan. So the group chief executive's letters will also initiate these exercises and are often aimed to assist in management decisions, such as diversification or divestment. They will often be concerned with financial aspects of strategies, such as leasing options. The latter can have group-wide ramifications; for instance if a division sells and leases back large assets there will be an impact upon the group's capital gearing. In many of the major exercises assistance will be needed from the corporate planning staff (in which case the guidelines letter will say so).

The contents of planning forms

Thirdly, when group chief executive's guidelines go out the group planning staff should provide the formats for each division to present its proposed strategy. The financial schedules are designed to ensure uniformity and financial conciseness in what is not a financial exercise (although its objectives and constraints may be set in financial terms). These schedules confine the data for each of the first five years to key variables such as turnover, operating profit, capital employed, working capital, capital and strategic expenditure, and cash flow, together with key ratios. If strategy proposals of individual businesses so dictate, further financial information can be included to amplify the text. Although in medium and large companies divisional planning staff are capable of providing the framework of strategic analysis and are familiar with the techniques discussed later in this chapter, the corporate planning function usually sets other guidelines for the divisional strategic plan formats. These guidelines may include such elements as:

- divisional financial objectives, expressed as return of capital and/or cash flow and which relate to the performance of competitors and 'look-alike' businesses in other industries,
- the amount of detail to be given to the key issues highlighted by the chief executive,
- methodology of the analysis of the relative competitive position of the core business,
- strategic options which should be considered by the division and which oblige the divisions to contemplate certain alternatives they might otherwise discard.

The divisional chief executives then set in train their own guidelines to provide each successive lower tier down to the SBUs with the information needed to formulate their strategic proposals. The proposals of the SBUs are the first to be formulated and these are carried out in consultation with their reporting tier. The consultation includes the dialogues needed to marshal and apply (via the feedback mechanism) the information the reporting tier needs to formulate its own proposals. Thus, at that stage a set of mutually consistent SBU proposals exists (provisional plans) consolidated into the proposals (provisional plan) of the next upper tier. Dialogues are essential but not enough on their own. They make possible effective decisions and control needed to arrive at proposals best fulfilling the strategic needs of the next higher tier, and so on up to those of the group. The chief executive at any level in the hierarchy is responsible for initiating and co-ordinating his own strategy development, assisted by his planning function.

The top-down review

While this bottom-up element of the strategic planning process is taking place, the start of the top-down process is initiated in January and should be completed by April, prior to the receipt of divisional plans at group level. The top-down review, initiated by the group chief executive and supported by his group board executive directors and corporate planning staff, examines:

- the group's financial objectives and constraints, namely: levels of profitability (earnings/shares) and rate of profit growth to be sought; limits of capital and income gearing within which the group should operate; likely dividend policy,
- the limited number of major strategic issues likely to be thrown up by the divisional plans, relating solely to the divisions and preparing the group to anticipate those issues,
- the group issues which may arise from a mismatch of top-down objectives and bottom-up strategies,
- the specific group issues concerning the type of company it wishes to be – factors such as the degree of decentralisation desirable and the level of central overhead, acquisition and divestment, long-term development or diversification.

Some of these matters may be decided upon fully by April, e.g. financial objectives, while others will require a full assessment of the divisional plans and will not be finally agreed until towards the end of the strategic planning process.

By the end of April the divisions are required to finalise the preparation of their proposed strategies and pass them to group level. The corporate planner's role now is to act as staff support for the group's executive directors, analysing the plans, putting each into a group perspective, spelling out the resultant strategic options open to the group and making a first approximation of a group consolidation. This involves writing a detailed report on each plan raising key questions about the soundness of the strategy, the likelihood of its achievement, and the claims for resources. Copies are sent to the respective division chief executives and to the group's executive directors. A meeting is held for each division, chaired by the group's chief executive, to discuss each plan in detail and in the light of an emerging group plan.

Allocating resources

This is the point where the group's pre-eminent constraints are brought fully into focus and where the ultimate determinants of the plan are delineated. The most obvious constraint is cash available for strategic development – the amount judged prudent to earmark through the development of the existing businesses, and from borrowing facilities. Given entrepreneurial thinking in the divisions, there is frequently a greater hunger for resources than ability to supply. The group chief executive then must determine what pattern of distribution resources is likely to achieve the best attainable strategy for the group. He will be guided by the results of the top-down corporate strategy deliberations as well as by the claims of the divisional strategies.

His provisional scheme of resource allocation and his recommendations on other key strategic constraints should now be highlighted as a set of documented issues. This is imperative as the final stage in the preparation of the strategic plan submission to the group's board. The final step is deliberation of the issues by the group chief executive and his executive directors leading to specific recommendations.

The staff work entailed in the highlighting and documentation should be carried out by the corporate planning staff, because they are required to incorporate the crucial arguments and decisions in the strategic document submitted to the board.

Comparing this problem of strategic allocation of resources in an intricate group with that in a one man business, gives a good idea of the range of problems of strategic planning. The end result has to be a clearly stated exposition of a strategy which it is intended to follow. In figure 6.2 that culmination happens in July when the group's board examines and finally decides on the strategic plan. Whatever the structure or size of a business, its chances of survival and growth are very much increased if it carries through a regular systematic planning exercise and handles information effectively.

The second half of the annual cycle harnesses similar principles of iterative processing to those in strategic planning. The essential difference lies in the nature of the information, which is tactical and tailored to suit the required end result – the production of that short term set of tactics and detailed financial statements which best accords with an effective pursuit of the organisation's objectives and strategy.

The group's budget (operating plan) programme is best begun with an individual letter from the group chief executive to each divisional chief executive in July, immediately after completing the review and update of the group strategy. Each letter should set out the guidelines to be followed. They include conclusions about each division reached by the group's directors. Although each divisional chief executive will have a copy of that document he will require the guidelines as well, to provide him with specific information about how the key conclusions should be translated into action.

Such formal letters and less formal discussions make each divisional chief executive clearly aware of (and able to accept) what his division is expected to achieve during the year by way of return on investment, generation of funds, and other criteria. The letter also confirms the level of core and strategic investment allocated to the division for the budget year.

The divisional chief executive must now let his own executives know (and accept in a similar manner) what is expected of them. The information has to be specifically tailored at every level so that everyone knows everything he needs to know. Every executive must be allocated stretching but not unattainable objectives, reached after discussion and information exchange throughout the division.

The time available for these interactions is short. The guidelines for SBUs are not finalised until the end of August, whereas draft budgets have to be ready for the beginning of the bottom-up dialogue a month or so later. For this reason the SBUs must begin their budget preparations in rough form and produce hard data such as production and marketing overheads for the forthcoming year as early as they can, before they receive their top-down master guidelines.

Highlights of the budgeting process

The main thrust of this chapter concerns strategic planning and the budgeting process is not described in detail but its main elements are outlined.

Far greater financial detail is required in the budget than in the strategic plan, because the consolidated budget is used as a yardstick to monitor the performance of every SBU and higher tier business. It must be formulated in a way which permits each component to be recognised. The inclusion of detailed projections in a strategic plan is likely to obscure important strategic issues, but the reverse applies to a budget. It is necessary to be much more precise about sales, costs, profits, working capital, fixed capital and investment proposals in the budget than in the strategy.

The nature of budgets makes it desirable for group finance to prescribe the formats in which it is to be compiled and the timetable to be followed. These instructions should be issued in July, immediately after the group chief executive's guideline letter. That function should also carry out all the consolidations at group level, and prepare an appropriate commentary including clear expositions of major variations between the budget and the first year of the strategic plan, taking into account the effects of the economic cycle. However, no change in the strategy itself should be contemplated in preparing the budget.

Every projection for budgets must be based on uniform environmental assumptions. Those issued earlier in the year for strategic plans need to be refined by the corporate planning function in the light of intervening developments.

The feeding down of information is followed rapidly by the feeding up process. The SBUs present draft budgets to their superiors in early October and agreement is reached at that level later in the month, and so on upwards. The divisions aim to finalise their proposals by the end of October or early November, for presentation at group level during November. It is very imporatant to note that this process, as in the case of the strategy exercise, must be co-ordinated in each division by one person, ideally the divisional chief executive. He should be present at all the sub-divisional and higher deliberations, making international trips if he is the executive responsible for foreign operations, all the while remaining in close touch with developments in the division's strategic thinking.

This top-down and bottom-up dialogue, with its attendant continuous exchange of information, should ultimately be consolidated into a set of group tactics and financial statements which provide acceptable objectives for the coming year. The group budget will have been scrutinised, amended and approved by the group's board during December. One of the most important issues resolved is the detailed allocation of capital and strategic expenditure to business for the coming year. These allocations will be clearly identified, with the intent that they will not be deviated from unless events intervene in ways which cannot be circumvented.

Conceptual techniques for planning

Techniques for planning fall into two principal categories: conceptual and analytical.

Conceptual techniques are designed to aid the perception of how an organisation should act in circumstances where courses of action cannot be solely derived from direct measures such as financial and economic data. Perhaps their most familiar application is in portfolio analysis, and its implications for resource allocation.

The most widely used methodology up to the early 1970s was the Boston Consulting Group's (BCG) famous 'Growth Share Matrix' which classifies business into the four categories of 'star', 'cash cow', 'question mark' and 'dog', according to the business's position relative to the two axes of market growth and relative market share. This simplistic system was useful in the expansionary epoch which ended in 1973 and BCG now advocate more subtle approaches, (Financial Times reports 1981). More detail is given in chapter 7.

Another more comprehensive conceptual aid, typically using a nine-celled matrix, was originated by General Electric and subsequently developed by McKinsey, Shell and others. This has been variously called 'The Company Position/Attractiveness Screen' and 'The Directional Policy Matrix' (DPM). The positions, and hence strengths, of businesses are plotted according to a range of criteria relating to the business itself along one axis, and set of criteria relating to the attractiveness of the industry to which it belongs along the other. Numerical 'scores' are allocated for each criterion to the business and to the industry. The criteria are weighted according to their relative importance. As there are ten or a dozen criteria relating to each axis, there is an almost infinite scope for judgemental differentiation. Nevertheless, the exercise helps engender a feel for the situation of each business (Robinson, Wade and Hichens, 1978). Nowadays it is highly unlikely any management would adopt a strategy based wholly on such conceptual aids. However, their use is preferable to guidance largely by hunch.

Analytical techniques for planning

There is an even wider range of analytical exercises from which to choose examples. The economic environmental documents belong to this category, but we will illustrate it by very brief descriptions of just two: PIMS and capital asset pricing.

PIMS is an organisation run by the Strategic Planning Society. Practically any company can become a subscription paying member and gain access to the PIMS database, provided it contributes a regular supply of comprehensive information about the SBU's products and marketplace. This information is in PIMS uniform format designed to enable about thirty key strategic variables to be calculated. Anonymity is protected. The strategic variables are defined in a precise and uniform way so that they can be assigned purely numerical values in multivariate regression equations. In the process each SBU is categorised by its strategic characteristics and not by the nature of its activities.

The PIMS results are based on the analysis of very large amounts of data; currently between two and three thousand SBUs of member companies are in the database. A significant number are in the UK and European countries, each yielding (usually annually) a value for the thirty or so key variables. Over the decade of its application many relationships of high statistical significance have been established between the variables. These relationships are said to constitute virtual 'laws of the marketplace' which can be of very great value to the subscribing members, provided they remember that other laws might emerge emanating perhaps in businesses outside the PIMS programme. They might also emerge from their own characteristics, for instance from the upheaval ensuing if established practices which work reasonably well are changed too abruptly. More information about the operation of PIMS is given in chapter 7.

Capital asset pricing is a method of estimating the cost of capital to a business organisation. There is a risk premium expected by the owners of every business over a risk-free form of investment such as three month Treasury bills. This premium has to be gauged by management to provide a measure of how the business should perform, and certainly in the private sector how it has got to perform to survive in the long run.

The minimum expected return on any public company's equity (which is the cost of its equity capital) is the rate of return on risk free securities plus the product of two risk-related factors, one specific to the company called its Beta, and another called 'the risk premium', common to all quoted companies. A company's Beta is an empirical measure of the market risk associated with its equity. The risk premium is the difference between the overall return on equities and the risk free return from Treasury bills and their like. All the numbers vary with time and the London Business School Risk Management Service regularly publishes its current assessment of the Betas for all companies quoted on the London Stock Exchange and also the concurrent overall risk premium.

The method can be applied to practically any business to give a close approximation of the cost of its equity capital, irrespective of whether or not it is a quoted company. All that is required for an unquoted business is to find a quoted company with a similar business and use that company's Beta for evaluation. The risk premium, of course, is directly applicable. It may not be easy to do and many quoted companies usually have to be examined to find a good 'look-alike'.

Bringing together the conceptual and analytical approaches, Porter (1980) assesses the strategic position of a business in relation to its strength versus its suppliers and customers as well as its competitors. The approach is perhaps the most comprehensive of those published and is recommended reading for all professional planners. In the past few years, global recession and uncertainty have caused many to question the validity of such systematic approaches. Some now feel that strategic lessons can best be learned by an examination of the strategies and policies of the most successful company (Peters and Waterman, 1983), or by seeking insights through studying the beneficial and unproductive aspects of corporate culture.

Order, analysis, iteration, perseverance

It has to be emphasised that every business has within itself all the information needed to determine its options under any environmental assumptions. The fundamental role of strategic planning is to elicit and organise this information to reveal the range of options and to demonstrate how preferrred options might be achieved.

This chapter is about that role and about how it can be approached in a rather complicated organisation. This is not a straightforward matter. It is not straightforward in a simple organisation either. Four essentials encapsulate the approach outlined:

Order — Order is the key to the organisation and processing of information.

Analysis	The analysis of ordered information reveals the crucial issues confronting any organisation.
Iteration	This is perhaps best illustrated by the process of repeated trial and error aimed at reaching an optimal solution, or goal, by successively better approximations.
Perseverance	There will inevitably be a very great deal of mutual conflict between the interests of different parts of the organisation. Only perseverance will uncover whatever innate mutuality or synergy the organisation possesses.

7 Specific planning techniques

John Fawn

Introduction

Planning in the 1950s and 1960s tended to be based on extrapolative forecasting and devising strategies to fill the planning gap created by the expected growth. Most companies operated in reasonably stable environments and extending the past was a realistic approach to life. As companies became more sophisticated they moved from one-year budgeting processes to three to five-year planning. Planning often 'extended' budgeting.

Simulation models were developed in the 1960s as an extension of this process. Increases in computer capability allowed construction of computer models which allowed 'what-if' questions to be asked.

During the 1960s the environment became more unstable. The stability of foreign exchange rates for instance was shattered by the devaluation of the reserve currencies, both sterling and the dollar. Inflation became an important factor.

Companies started to look for strategic frameworks to enable them to make sense of their 'bottom-up' budgeting planning techniques. The demand was initially satisfied by consultancy groups who developed methodologies which allowed a logical overview of the use of top-down approaches. To be fair to the consultancy groups, they then used these top-down approaches in conjunction with the companies' budgeting processes to provide a highly professional strategy guidance service.

Analysis tools

This chapter sets out some of the more useful approaches that have been developed. Some approaches were quantitative. Some were complicated and some were simple. It is worth exploring some of the techniques in each area as they are useful and different analysis tools. Nobody developed a simple qualitative method, perhaps because this is what the chief executive had relied on for so long. One of each of the major approaches coincides with the quadrants of the matrix in Figure 7.1.

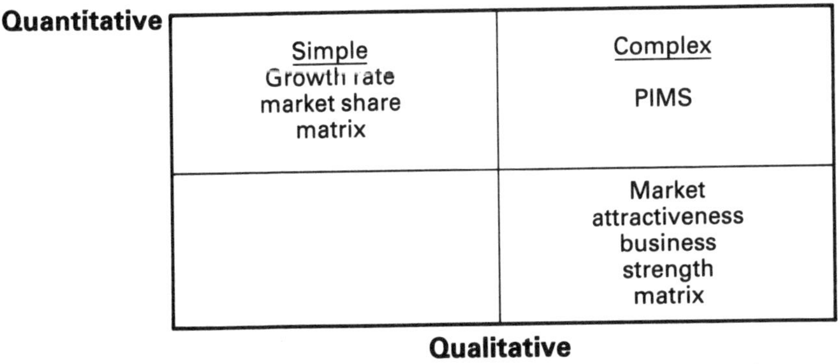

Quantitative		
	Simple Growth rate market share matrix	Complex PIMS
		Market attractiveness business strength matrix
	Qualitative	

Figure 7.1 Analysis tools

The growth rate – market share matrix (GRMS matrix)

One of the most successful companies with a simple quantitative methodology was the Boston Consultancy Group (BCG) who developed the BCG (the growth rate – market share) matrix. Boston Consulting Group concepts developed in the 1960s and 1970s and were based on the premises:

(a) all costs will fall, as experience in providing a product or services increases,
(b) empirical evidence suggests that costs will fall by a constant factor each time experience doubles,
(c) this concept is known as the experience or learning curve,
(d) if the learning factor is 0.9, then the progress will be:

No. of Units	*Costs of last units compared with first unit*
1	1.00
2	0.90
4	0.81
8	0.73
16	0.66
64	0.59
.	
.	
.	
.	
1024	0.39

Learning curve factors as low at 0.8 can operate on a continuous basis. The learning curve is based on observations in the aircraft industry during the Second World War. In that environment learning factors of 0.86 for machined components and 0.83 for component assembly were expected.

If all companies are able to manage their operations down the same learning curve, the company with the greatest experience will have the lowest costs and hence the highest profits. Experience is essentially a measure of volume, and the company with the highest market share will have the greatest volume. If the company with the highest market share is properly managed, it will have the greatest profitability.

Market share is important and one must devise a strategy to become market leader. Analysis of a typical product life cycle indicates that growth is highest in the early stages of life. It is easier in fast-growing markets to increase absolute market share since it is not necessary to remove business from competitors to gain market share. In addition the volumes of business are smaller early in the product life cycle, and if it is necessary to 'buy' market share, this is the cheapest time to do it. See figure 7.2.

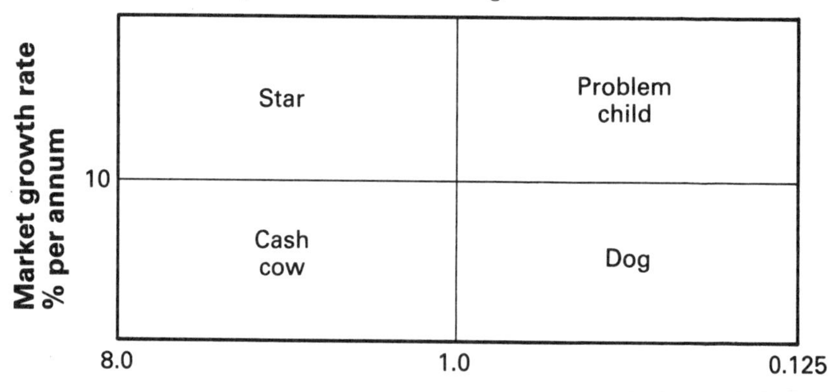

Figure 7.2 Growth rate – market share matrix

The X axis, indicates the market share of the company in a given market segment relative to the market leader. In the case of the market leader, the position is expressed relative to the second largest company. An index of 1.0 or greater indicates market leadership. The further to the left on the axis, the greater the market share. The scale is logarithmic.

The Y axis indicates the percentage growth per annum for the given product market segment. The horizontal line is usually drawn at 10%, but this figure is somewhat arbitrary.

Analysing a portfolio of businesses

The growth rate – market share matrix is at its most useful when used to analyse a portfolio of businesses. It allows the corporate headquarters a framework against which to judge the different areas of diverse business.

To plot its portfolio, a company must:

(a) define the appropriate product market segment in which each of its businesses competes,
(b) identify the competitors in each product's market segment,
(c) establish the market growth rate and the market shares of all competing companies.

The positions on the X and Y axes can then be established. The relative sizes of businesses in a portfolio can be portrayed by drawing circles at the appropriate point, the area of the circle representing the level of the sales revenue.

Interpreting the matrix

The analysis characterises each of the four segments in the diagram.

1 Businesses in the lower left-hand segment are termed cash cows. These businesses are market leaders in relatively slow-growth segment maturing industries. As such they should be generators of cash which should be used to support high-growth business.

2 Businesses in the lower right-hand segment are termed dogs. These businesses are not market leaders and are operating in low growth segments where expanding a market share means that someone else will lose volume. To gain market share from the competition will probably be very expensive since aggressive action in the market place is likely to lead to fighting responses. The risk of such businesses is that they will consume cash and still not improve their market share position.

3 Businesses in the upper left-hand segment are known as stars. These businesses are market leaders in high growth segments. Leadership must be maintained. This will inevitably require cash to increase capacity, distribution facilities, and so on. As market growth slows, these businesses will drop into the lower left-hand segment, thus today's stars are tomorrow's cash cows.

4 Businesses in the upper right-hand segments are known as question marks or problem children. They are good in that they are in fast growth markets, but bad in that they are not market leaders. To prevent them from becoming future dogs they must be moved to the left to become stars. This is likely to require significant amounts of cash. Major strategic decisions may be required in that a company might only have sufficient resources to fund a limited number of the existing problem children. There is a major risk in trying to fund too many problem children all at an inadequate level. Selectivity should produce some stars and some withdrawal/divestments. Failure to make a choice might produce only dogs.

Construction of the matrix should lead to the following questions:

(a) Does the company have an appropriate number of cash generators?
(b) Does the company have an appropriate number of stars? Are these being adequately funded to ensure they remain market leaders and so become future cash cows?
(c) How many problem children can be funded to the extent that they can become stars? The high growth period in the product life cycle is the time when it is easiest to obtain market leadership. Should some problem children be sold?
(d) Are dogs being allowed to consume cash? Should disposals take place?

Cash must not flow from cash cows to dogs. It must flow to stars and to selected problem children.

Plotting the portfolio year by year and superimposing the charts will show the 'direction' of movement for each business, showing whether the 'structure' of the portfolio is improving over time. Plotting the company growth rate against industry growth rate over time gives an indication of direction on the matrix. Extending the plots into the future and justifying a change in direction (e.g. losing market share in the past to increasing market share in the future) is also a valuable exercise.

Plotting the portfolio of major competitors may give guidance on their strategic action, e.g. heavy funding of stars, disposal of dogs. It may also suggest areas of weakness to attack vigorously.

Problems associated with the GRMS matrix analysis

The growth rate – market share matrix is a useful concept which is easy to understand. It does have major difficulties which can lead a company to take wrong decisions if the concept is used without understanding. In a complex business world it is most unlikely that just two variables will be adequate as a basis on which to take decisions.

Easily identified difficulties lie in the areas of data, conceptual invalidity and companies that do not play to the rules.

Data

Accurate/appropriate definition of product market segments can be subjective and may be very difficult to establish. Within the definitions decided, market size and share for one's own company may be difficult to quantify. Obtaining the same information for competitors may be impossible. Even the total market growth rates may not be available for the specific segment, particularly if that segment does not coincide with a national standard definition.

Conceptual invalidity
The experience curve concept is empirical and may not always be appropriate, for example in cases of low labour costs, exceptional degree of plant capacity utilisation, major technology changes, or access to favourable supplies. Government regulations affect market dominance in such forms as monopoly legislation and price control.

Companies that don't play to the rules
Duopolies may be very profitable for the smaller supplier. Very mature markets may profitably support several competitors all in the 'flat' part of the experience curve. Small companies may prosper in particular industry segments by specifically not playing the 'competitive game' of the large companies in the industry. The concept of economies of scale on which the growth rate – market share matrix is based can be overcome by either establishing a market niche, or by the concept of small is beautiful.

Profit impact of marketing strategy (PIMS)

The fundamental concept of the PIMS model is that certain characteristics of a business and its market determine profitability. Understanding these characteristics and acting upon them will aid a company with its unique attributes to become more profitable.

The PIMS project is a multivariate regression model which seeks to determine those variables which most significantly affect return on investment and cash flow. It is claimed that the model can account for over 80% of the variation of profitability on the basis of 37 variables (or 60% on the basis of 18 variables). As such it can be assessed as being both complex and quantitative.

The General Electric Corporation of the USA initiated the project. They wondered whether it would be possible by analysing their many operations to identify those factors which made the business successful. As the project grew it was taken over by the Harvard Business School. In 1975, the Strategic Planning Institute, a non-profit making corporation governed by the member companies was formed to manage the PIMS project. By the early 1980s over 200 companies operating more than 2,000 businesses contributed. Most of the companies are from outside the United States.

Each contributing company is asked to fill in a very detailed questionnaire requiring financial information and judgement. Initally information is required over a 5-year time period.

Updates are required each year and as time goes by a very complete data base evolves. Experience in Britain indicates that when a company first joins, the effort required to generate the required information is enormous and, when the first company analysis is returned the process is repeated because the results can be uncomfortable. The variables used can be grouped in five main headings.

1. Attractiveness of market environment
   - long run (4 - 10 years ahead) industry growth rate
   - short run (up to 3 years ahead) industry growth rate
   - stage in the product life cycle
2. Strength of competitive position
   - market share
   - relative product quality
   - relative breadth of product line
3. Effectiveness of use of investment
   - investment intensity (total investment/sales; also total investment/value added)
   - fixed capital intensity (fixed capital/sales)
   - vertical integration (value added/sales)
   - percent capacity utilised
4. Discretionary budget allocations
   - market expense/sales
   - research and development expense/sales
   - new product expense/sales
5. Current changes in market position
   - change in market share

Company confidentiality is respected by a process known as sanitising the data. It allows analysis of the data base by individual companies, because it makes identification of information sources very difficult. The model is used at three separate levels.

1. Determining the major factors which affect the ROI of a business. Analysis at this level is possible by using the model to illustrate how two or three variables interrelate by fixing all the other variables at a constant level.
2. Analysing a company's performance relative to PAR values to establish its strengths and weaknesses.
3. Assessing the implications of strategic changes, including indications of promising strategies for improving the ROI and cash flow of a given business.

The model shows the impact of a single variable or a pair of variables on ROI and cash flows.

The major determinants of ROI appear from analysis as:

1 capital intensity
2 market share
3 market growth
4 life cycle stage
5 marketing expense/sales ratio

Notice that factors 2, 3 and 4 are the variables used in the growth rate – market share matrix. The PIMS model shows up some myths in the folklore of running a business.

The impact of capital intensity

It has long been argued by capital-intense industries that the cost of getting into such a business creates barriers to entry which should maintain profitability. The problem with capital-intense industries is that increments in capacity tend to come in large units and if more than one company decides to make an investment the industry utilisation is bound to suffer. PIMS findings indicate that:

- The larger the capital intensity (investment/sales) the lower the ROI. Large investment and high marketing intensity produces poor ROI.
- Capacity utilisation is vital when fixed capital intensity is high.
- High capital intensity and small market share cause disaster.
- Low or medium growth coupled with low capital intensity produces cash. High growth coupled with high capital intensity produces a cash drain.
- Harvesting market share when capital intensity is low produces cash. Building market share when capital intensity is high is a cash drain.

From these statements it is possible to construct yet another matrix with which one can judge a company's performance, as in Figure 7.3.

The definition of market share is the same as in the growth rate – market share matrix.

The impact of market share and growth rate

Market share has always been considered one of the major parameters for a successful company. PIMS confirms this:

- ROI is closely related to relative market share.
- Market share is most profitable in vertically integrated industries.
- High R & D spending depresses ROI when market share is weak.

- Capacity utilisation is most important for low share businesses.
- Market share and quality are partial substitutes for each other.
- High relative market share improves cash flow, especially when marketing intensity is low. High growth decreases it. (Growth Rate – Market Share justification).

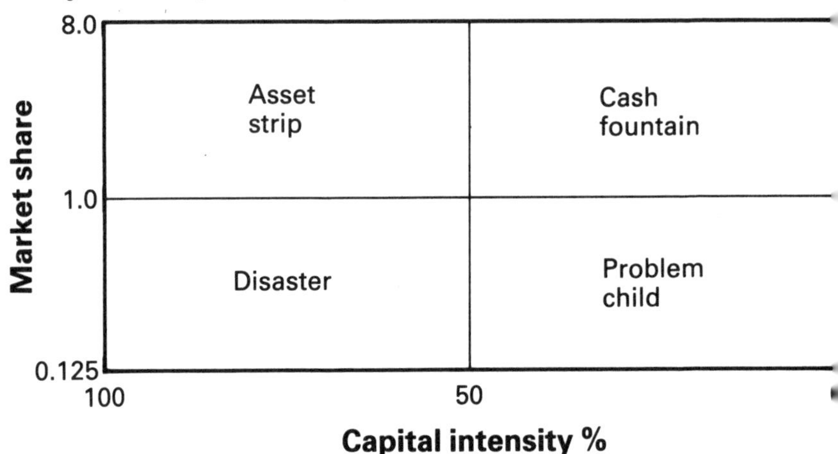

Figure 7.3 Capital intensity – market share matrix

One of the interesting observations in this list is the substitution ability of market share and quality. It allows that product differentiation is a reasonable strategy to follow.

Ansoff (1984) identifies three types of product life cycle: stable, fertile and turbulent. As the market develops he identifies that it is in the early stages of growth that product innovation is at its most critical. He observes that money can be made at the early growth stage only on stable technology products. With fertile technology (rapid incremental product development within the same technology) and turbulent technology (product replacement with a new technology) the investment required in product development precludes profitability. PIMS confirms this in that:

- A rapid rate of new product introduction in fast-growing markets depresses ROI.
- R & D is most profitable in mature slow-growth markets.

More conclusions can be drawn from PIMS at this level. It is inherently valuable to be able to evaluate the probable success of different strategies. through PIMS.

PAR value comparison

The next level of PIMS allows a company to evaluate its performance against industry average. If there are any marked differences PIMS will attempt to identify which factors are causing the deviations. For a company with a diverse portfolio of products it is unrealistic to expect an equal rate of return and such information as 'PAR' gives allows a much more realistic evaluation.

Assessing the implications of strategic change

PIMS at this level has several options. The first is a prediction of what the effect of a change of strategy would have on the company performance. There is a major worry in this work that these outputs might be misleading because it is necessary to think through all of the inter-related factors when making changes.

Another capability is the 'Optimum Strategy Report' which predicts which combinations of strategic moves result in the best ROI or cash flow.

In all cases such reports must be understood in the context of the actual business. It is highly dangerous to accept the conclusions without due consideration. Perhaps the best advice to those using such information is 'Don't ignore what the model says but don't believe what the model says either'.

Conclusions on PIMS

Many criticisms of the PIMS project have been voiced:

Is short term ROI the best measure for judging a business? In western cultures where shareholder interests have tended to be paramount, this is one of the more highly regarded measures of success. In other cultures, such as Japan, where the equity is much more locally owned by the proprietors and workforce, and money is raised through long term debt, other measures are used which tend to be much longer term. There can be no denying that such cultures seem to be at least as successful as the traditional Western industry approach.

The model is based on historic data and largely ignores future changes. In a world of discontinous change, extrapolation into the future is always dangerous. On the other hand, the models of successful change available indicate that it is possible to change direction only gradually, and that the successful companies are successful because they stick to doing what they know best.

Synergy between separate businesses in the organisation (if it can be defined mathematically or even if it exists) is ignored. The data base is generated from companies, many of whom are in diverse but related businesses where a synergy effect ought to be measurable.

The process is highly analytical but very limited in solving problems – it can be accused of being a tool with which academics can try out their theories, but not one which can be used as a framework within which strategies can be built. There is a major problem for a practising manager in using the process. It is a very complex system with many of the variables in the model highly inter-dependent. The statistical errors in the findings are very rarely discussed at management level and output risks the 'black box syndrome', meaning that because of the complexity, it must be right because the computer says so.

Finally many of the factors which the model says control the fate of a company are outside the control of the managers of that company. Knowing that the model says you are doomed is not helpful.

There are major problems with using the output from PIMS and only some of the larger companies use it. It is important as an approach, however, because it is the only major data base of this nature in existence. All other top-down approaches to planning start by using a theory which cannot be proved scientifically (unless by using PIMS) and then hang strategies on the framework that has been generated. PIMS starts from saying 'Let us see what we can learn from quantitative business data'.

Market attractiveness – business strength matrix

Many companies tried to develop a qualitative methodology for evaluating a company's strategic position and recommending possible strategic directions. The simple growth rate – market share method, while being attractive, was felt to exclude the major variables which make each business individual.

A reasonable distillation of this process is the market attractiveness – business strength matrix. Market growth is replaced by market attractiveness. This in turn can include a wide range of variables determined by the individual company such as:

market size,
market growth rate, both historic and projected,
cyclicality,
seasonality,
number of competitors and degree of industry concentration,
number of entrants and exits in past five years,
industry return on capital,
barriers to entry,
capacity utilisation,

maturity of industry technology,
extent of patent protection,
degree of government regulations affecting industry,
attitude of society to industry.

Relative market share is replaced by business strength. This can include variables such as:

absolute and relative market share,
historic return on capital,
achieved margins,
strength of product line,
strength of distribution channels,
security of raw material supplies,
patents held,
R & D capability,
managerial capability.

It is argued that each of these factors has a major influence on the strategic direction of a company. The exact effect however varies from industry to industry. R & D capability for instance ought to have a greater weighting in the electronics industry than in a service industry. The first job of the planner is therefore to weight the individual factors subjectively for his industry.

Once the appropriate variables have been selected, each business in the portfolio must be evaluated. This requires a single value or score for each matrix axis for the separate businesses. Since variables included can be both quantitative and qualitative and have varying importance, the process involves much subjective judgement on the part of the planner.

Each business is plotted on the matrix. Again, direction can be assessed by using historic and future plots. In strategic terms the matrix is generally interpreted as shown in Figure 7.4.

The method is an extremely powerful portfolio tool and is used by many companies and consultancies. One of the major advantages to this comparatively complex procedure is that it forces the analysts to question the fundamental bases of the business. One of the more enlightening things, having evaluated the company's portfolio of business, is to do so for major competitors. It may well be possible to evolve business strategies which minimise conflicts of interests.

Businesses in the upper left-hand part of the matrix are growth areas which should attract investment. Businesses in the lower right-hand part should be questioned as to their viability. Those ranging from lower left to upper right require careful selective investment decisions or a policy of harvesting cash from them.

Market Attractiveness	Hi (Competitive position)		Lo (Competitive position)
Hi	Grow Penetrate	Invest for growth	Selective investment or divestment
	Selective harvest or investment	Segment and selective investment	Controlled exit or divestment
Lo	Harvest for cash generation	Controlled harvest	Rapid exit or attack business

Figure 7.4 Market attractiveness – business strength matrix

The major criticism of the market attractiveness – business strength matrix is the subjectivity involved in selecting the variables to be included in weighting their importance. There is always the temptation to re-evaluate or discredit the figures if the answeres are unpalatable. Attempts to overcome this problem have been the subject of several PIMS projects. From a broad-based study, it does not seem that the weightings for different industries are significantly different. More work is being done on this, and for a larger number of industries.

Acceptance of planning techniques

Planning techniques are potentially very attractive to senior executives at corporate headquarters for the following reasons:

1. They give control back to top management. As companies grew larger and became more diverse, power probably shifted to divisional chief executives. The techniques described bring it firmly back to corporate HQ.
2. They enable rational decisions to be made. Top management can justify their decisions particularly to businesses which are to be run down/ divested.
3. Resource allocation (particularly capital) between totally diverse activities can be solved.

Top-down planning techniques cannot be used in isolation. Messages received from any particular technique are only indications. If the same message is received from several techniques, that message starts to gain credibility. The methodology of the top-down process allows, or even forces, a detached but objective view of a business.

Decisions should not be taken on information provided solely from planning in a top-down mode. The beginning of this chapter described how planning evolved from the budgeting (bottom-up) process. Strategies evolved from matching the top-down and bottom-up processes are the ones most likely to be well thought out and acceptable for implementation. Recent developments in spreadsheet technologies allow much more flexibility in trying alternatives out. The way forward in planning methodology appears to be in the ability to do scenario planning from both a top-down and bottom-up approach.

I wish to thank Professor C.J. Constable, Director of the Cranfield School of Management, for his help in creating this chapter.

8 Corporate planning and the management accountant

David Allen

The shift towards strategy

It is now almost a cliché to talk about the turbulence which characterises the environment in which both private and public enterprise must operate. This turbulence results from the coming together of various forces which impact on the enterprise.

The predominant progressive forces, i.e. those setting the pace of change, are two-fold:

- technical (witness the enormous strides being made in computers, telecommunications, robotics, biotechnology)
- economic (witness the deregulation of prices, exchange decontrol, fluctuating exchange rates, financial futures markets)

Set against these are the reactionary forces, i.e. those tending to resist change, namely social and political, which are the basis for restrictive practices, security of employment agreements, redundancy compensation legislation and the whole panoply of government intervention in the economy through taxes and subsidies. These factors are summarised in Figure 8.1.

The consequence of all of this turbulence is that the outcome of decisions has become considerably more uncertain, but the penalty for wrong decisions more severe. Management attention has shifted from the tactical level of control (how well are we doing what we chose to do) to the strategic level (the choice of what to do). Thanks to computers and telecommunications taking over much of the calculation and presentation load at the operational and tactical levels (e.g. standard costing and budgetary control) management accountants have been able to respond to this exciting trend; to play a crucial role in strategic management. Under this heading are classified such issues as:

- acquisitions and divestment
- research and development
- expansion and diversification
- location of production facilities
- quality assurance
- economies of scale
- marketing investment

They have a major impact on the long-term health of the business.

Observation suggests that businesses evolve in stages, from extrapolative planning through awareness of the key external pressures and anticipation of changes therein, to the point where change is seen as an opportunity to seek a competitive advantage.

Almost by definition, the stakes, in terms of success or failure, are much higher at the strategic level. It follows that appraisal and control techniques must be correspondingly more powerful.

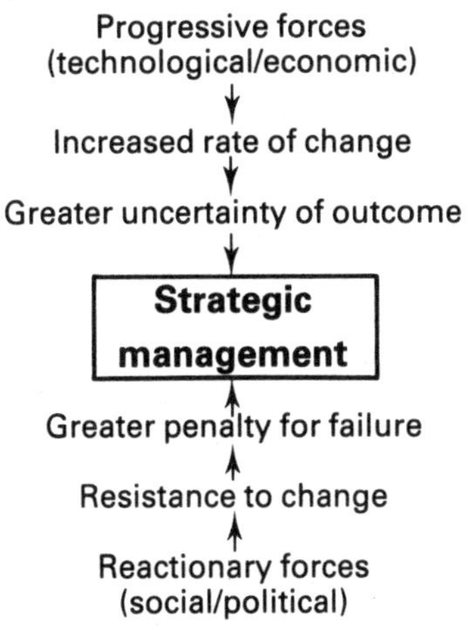

Figure 8.1 Environmental turbulence

Inadequacy of orthodox financial reports

What has become increasingly clear, however, is that orthodox financial reports are just not appropriate to the tasks of evaluating strategic alternatives and measuring strategic attainment. This should not be suprising: accounting concepts, after all, are geared to stewardship reporting, not decision making and control. Specifically:

- Accounts are backward looking; whereas decision making is a forward looking process. In stable conditions this might not be too much of a problem but in turbulent times, the past is obviously not a reliable guide to the future.
- Accounts are completely inward looking, whereas decision making must be substantially outward looking. Survival in a changing environment demands a heightened awareness of external trends, and the flexibility to adapt accordingly.
- Accounts are based on costs, whereas decision making is concerned with values. Managers do not embark on a particular course of action because they like the look of its cost, but because they expect the outcome to be worth more than cost. Thanks to the prudence concept, accountants treat many outlays as costs which managements see as investments (e.g. product development, training, advertising). To the decision maker such outlays are no different, fundamentally, from those which accountants treat as creating an asset, e.g. capital expenditure.
- Accounts are related to short-term discrete time periods, whereas decision making must be concerned with the longer-term continuum. A deep-seated malaise may well not be apparent in the accounts until it is too late to do anything about it.
- Accounts are expressed in terms of profits and assets employed, and are based on the concept of capital maintenance (though the debate surrounding the subject of accounting for changing price levels has shown just how nebulous this concept is). Resource allocation decisions, on the other hand, are viewed in terms of cash flows, the criterion being the cost of financing those flows (the cost of capital). The contrasts between accounting and decision-making needs are shown in figure 8.2.

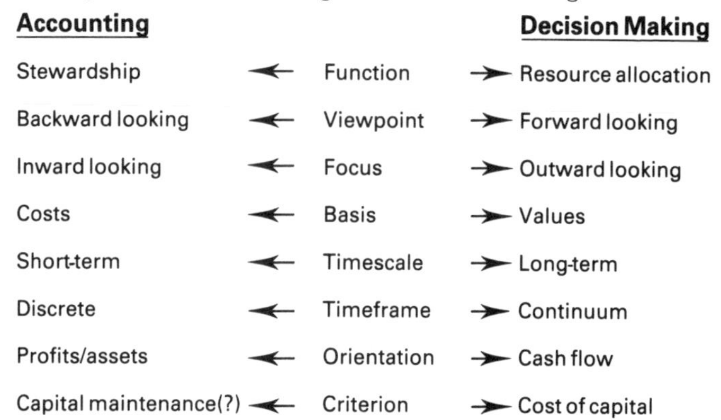

Figure 8.2 Contrasts – accounting and decision making

Some businesses claim to use discounted cash flow evaluations when making capital expenditure decisions (though few apply the technique to revenue investment or working capital). Rational feedback is precluded, however, because subsequent performance measurement is expressed in terms of reported profits – or some derivative thereof, such as return on capital.

Even more prevalent, however, are the businesses which pay no more than lip service to discounted cash flow evaluations, and consciously adopt return-on-capital as the basis for setting objectives, measuring performance and even remunerating executives. 'Stock Exchange pressures' are generally put forward for this emphasis and certainly the circumstantial evidence supports the contention. Brokers' circulars, the comments of financial journalists, and the Accounting Standards programme, do seem to be preoccupied with backward looking measures, typified by the earnings per share. Little wonder, then, that many Board meetings are dominated by the question 'are we on course for the profits expected by the City?'

The risk inherent in this situation is that managers will be tempted to follow a course of action which 'improves' current profits, even if it is at the expense of future profits, i.e. damages the long-term health of the business. If this year's return on capital is seen as the overriding objective, it will always appear preferable to chase low-margin business to put through underutilised facilities, rather than face the high front-end outlays (investment on both capital and revenue account) associated with adapting those facilities to the real needs of the market place. Failure is shored-up, and opportunities are neglected, leading to an undisclosed weakening of the business in terms of its ability to face the future.

In short, as indicators of the long-term health of a business, or of a subdivision thereof, accounting reports not only have little positive value, but – worse – can also be seriously misleading. Other things being equal, a shrinking business will always show better returns on capital than an expanding one. With such a measuring system the likelihood of resources being misdirected is just too great to be ignored. To combat this, there is a clear need for an approach which measures, for a business and its constituent activities, long-term financial health at a point in time, and the progress therein over time.

The structure of decision making

In addition to the changed nature of decision making outlined above, there has also been a fundamental shift in the process of decision making. Again, this shift has its roots in the rapid rate of change, this time through the sheer diversity which results. Centralised structures have experienced information-overload: the inability to respond to all the messages they receive.

Everywhere, the trend is towards decentralisation of authority and a broadening of the base of involvement in decision making. With a few obvious exceptions (namely employee buy-outs) enterprises stop short of creating autonomous units. The emphasis is on participation and interdependence: 'small within big is beautiful' sums up the philosophy; a network of micro-computers provides the physical manifestation.

Needless to say, this trend has rendered the old orthodoxy of control obsolete. Gone are the days (see Figure 8.3) of the top-down approach, where the Board set the strategy, middle management translated that into tactics, and first-line managers were punished if actual results varied from expectations. The terminology of budgetary control – classifying variances as favourable or adverse – is a living reminder of that approach.

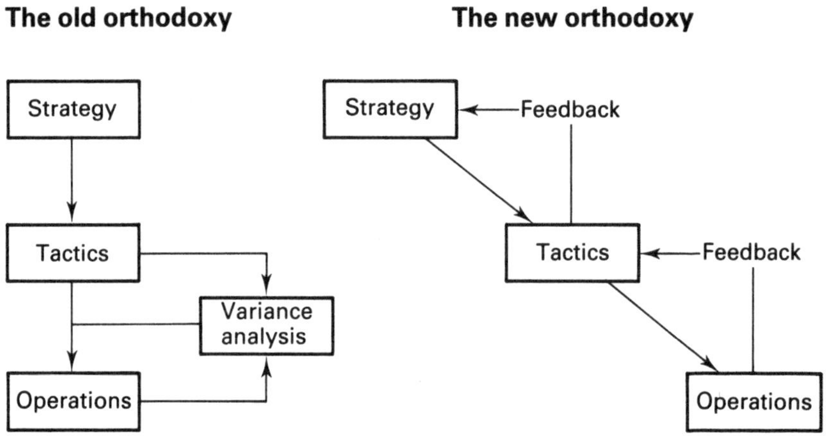

The old orthodoxy

Strategy
Tactics
Variance analysis
Operations

The new orthodoxy

Strategy
Feedback
Tactics
Feedback
Operations

Figure 8.3 Approaches to control

Enlightened managements, however, have moved to a new orthodoxy, based on the concept of a control loop. Here, variances are seen as signals that perhaps conditions are not in line with those assumed when the plan (strategy or budget) was formulated. If cash flows are greater than anticipated because of the postponement of a product launch, an advertising campaign or an acquisition of plant, can this really be described as favourable?

As part of the process of overhauling our techniques to fit them for the prevailing environment, we need to understand this new orthodoxy. Figure 8.4 supplies a schematic representation, which will now be amplified in the context of the strategic level of management.

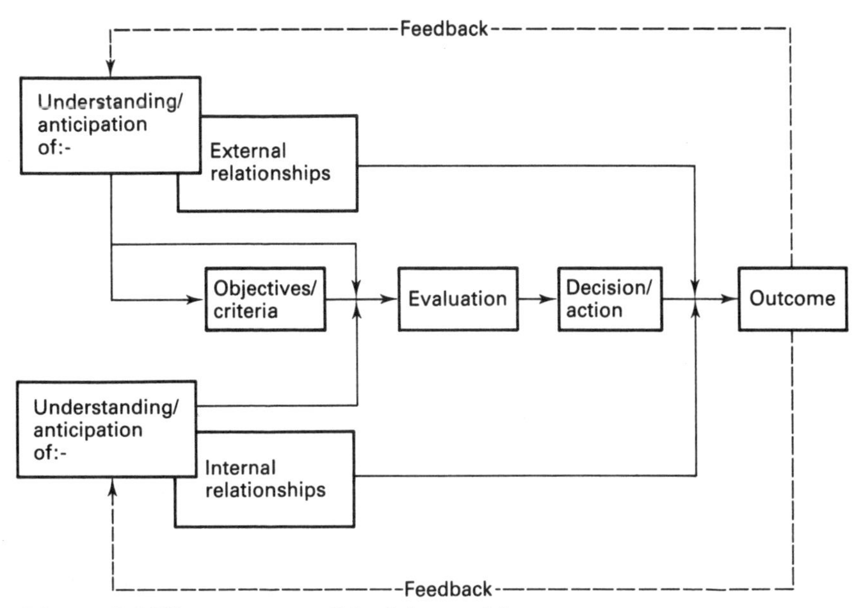

Figure 8.4 The structure of decision making

The easiest place to start is bottom-left with the understanding/anticipation of internal relationships. Most management information systems concentrate on this sector, and in general are quite effective. A typical internal relationship is cost/volume, for example, represented in cost accounting by the distinction between fixed and variable costs. Any cost accountant worthy of the title can give a sufficiently accurate answer to the question 'if volume throughout increases by 10% what is the likely increase in cost?'

Proficiency in the top-left sector, however, is very rare. In a rapidly changing environment, an understanding/awareness of external relationships is clearly paramount. Questions such as 'What is the likely increase in volume if we reduce prices by 10%, or double our advertising spend?' are increasingly relevant and important, but few management information systems are geared to supplying the answer.

One very special external relationship is the cost of capital. Almost by definition, strategic decisions are rarely focused on the profit statement alone. They usually have an impact on the balance sheet, and of course on cash flow. Whether that 10% price reduction makes sense, for example, boils down to whether the incremental profit (higher volume more than compensating for lower margins) provides an adequate return on the incremental investment (working capital to support the higher volume). What is adequate in this context depends on the returns expected by the suppliers of capital to the enterprise – usually a mixture of equity and borrowings.

At this point, the decision maker has views on the likely consequences of alternative courses of action. Spending money on advertising, for example, will generate expectations of volume and revenue increases, with consequent (though no doubt proportionally smaller) increases in costs, and assets employed. These projections can be evaluated in terms of incremental outlays and revenues, then discounted back to a net present value. The most positive option is the financially preferable one.

The outcome of the decision is a result of its interaction with the actually prevailing (as distinct from the anticipated) internal and external relationships. Any variance from expectation is therefore attributable to 'errors' in those anticipations. Because volumes increased less than anticipated, or costs increased more than anticipated, for example, the net present value of incremental cash flows is less than expected – perhaps even negative.

Analysing the key elements of outcome versus expectations provides a feedback which improves the decision making process. Perhaps our volume projections underestimate competitive reaction, perhaps our cost projections underestimated the militancy of trade unions, perhaps our cost of capital projections underestimated the capital market's support for our plans? Whatever the reason, it is worth knowing!

But how many financial control systems are structured to compare actual (or a later projection of) net present value with that which justified embarking on the particular strategy in question? Not many. Most seem to assume that reported profits are a measure of performance.

Yet the analysis clearly provides a framework within which to answer the fundamental question – how to measure long-term financial health and the progress therein – and to provide a measure of strategic attainment. The value of a business is a function of its anticipated cash flows, distilled into a net present value. If profit is meant to represent an increase in value, then tracking NPV is preferable to the accounting concepts we have inherited.

Financial objectives and criteria

In order to track NPV, it is necessary to picture financial management, particularly at the strategic level, as two distinct aspects: external and internal. The external aspect, usually referred to as the treasury function, is concerned with:

- the identification of the sources of funds, i.e. borrowing, grants or equity,
- the quantification of the corresponding expected rewards: interest, tax, and dividends,

- the mixing of the sources in a way which minimises the overall average requirement or cost of capital.

Meanwhile, the internal aspect, usually referred to as the financial control function, is concerned with:

- the definition of measurable activities (products/markets) with the business,
- the anticipation of outlays and revenues from each,
- the allocation of rescources to those activities offering the prospect of a return in excess of the cost of capital.

Thus the link between the two aspects is cost of capital: what the treasurer sees as the return necessary to warrant the employment of funds, the controller sees as the criterion for their deployment. This implies a unifying financial objective which can be expressed as the maximisation of the net present value of prospective cash flows, discounted at the cost of capital.

The treasurer concentrates on minimising the discount rate, the controller concentrates on maximising cash flows.

Say the cost of capital is projected at a steady 20% per annum. The controller evaluates projects by asking, in effect, 'Could we borrow money at 20% per annum, pay the appropriate interest, and still have a net surplus at the end of the project?'

	Absolute Cash Flows – £000s				*Discounted*
Year	*Capital Expenditure*	*Benefits*	*Net*	*20% Discount Factor*	*Cash Flows £000s*
1	(1000)	240	(760)	.833	(633)
2			280	.694	194
3			320	.579	185
4			360	.482	173
5			400	.402	161
	Final surplus				80

Figure 8.5 Archetypal viable project

Figure 8.5 shows the profile of a typical project which passes such a test. Cash is absorbed in the first year (e.g. on investing in plant and equipment) and generated in later years (e.g. through labour savings or extra volume). Discounting the various cash flows at 20% per annum produces a net present value of £80,000, and the project is classified as viable.

Assume now that this project is approved, and implemented, and the outcome is in line with expectations, how will it affect those traditional measures of performance: profits, assets employed, and hence return on capital?

Accounting conventions are such that the plant will be capitalised at £1 million, initially, then written down by way of a depreciation charge of £200,000 per annum (which will be deducted from the cash flow benefits to produce incremental profit figures). Figure 8.6 summarises this process over the five years of the project.

Year *£000s*	*1*	*2*	*3*	*4*	*5*	*Aggregate*
Assets employed	1000	800	600	400	200	3000
Contribution	240	280	320	360	400	1600
Depreciation	200	200	200	200	200	1000
Profit	40	80	120	160	200	600
% Return on assets	4	10	20	40	100	20

Figure 8.6 Accounting treatment

Notice particularly how the incremental profit increases (partly inflationary?) while the asset value decreases producing a very wide range of incremental returns.

Assume the business has a large number of similar projects, maturing at even rate. It would settle down at a rate of return of 20% per annum ignoring the impact of growth and inflation.

But, of course, we cannot ignore growth and inflation for more than a moment, and this is the whole point. A business which is growing has proportionately more activities in the first one or two years of life and shows a lower average return across all its activities.

Likewise, a company which is just keeping up with inflation has a proportionately greater money-value associated with projects in their first one or two years of life. It will show a lower return than one which is only maintaining the money-value of capital.

Other things being equal, a company which is shrinking will show a higher return on capital than a stable or growing one. Conversely, a management which is motivated by return on capital will have a bias towards contraction.

Expansion almost invariably induces front-end outlays, research and development, plant, training and marketing which have an adverse impact on key ratios.

This is not to say that return on capital is devoid of usefulness. It is a valid measure of the quality of past investment (though the vagaries of inflation make the actual measurement very complex). The point is that it is not a guide to current performance. The management in the example would see the project in question as having an adverse effect on apparent performance for two years. To counteract this bias we need to focus on cash flows.

The primacy of cash flow

Identifying the two aspects of financial management – external and internal – is important, so is understanding cash flow.

Externally, the relationship between an enterprise and the capital market is summed up in its cash flow. If new investment (in the form of loans, grants, or equity) exceeds distribution (interest, tax and dividends, respectively) then the enterprise is a net absorber of funds. Conversely, if distributions exceed investment it is a net generator.

Internally, the relationship between an enterprise and its constituent activities – usually product/market business units – is also focused on cash flow. Activities which are expanding faster than can be financed from their own profits are seen as absorbers of funds. Those whose profits are more than sufficient to finance their own expansion are seen as generators.

Investment + Retentions	=	Expansion
∴ Retentions	=	Expansion - Investment
i.e. Profit - Distribution	=	Expansion - Investment
or Profit - Expansion	=	Distributions - Investment
i.e. Profit - Expansion	=	Cash flow
or Profit	=	Cash flow + Expansion

Figure 8.7 Funds flow algebra

The interrelationships of these two aspects are highlighted in Figure 8.7. Moving roughly clockwise around the network, it can be seen that external investment, augmented by retentions, funds the operating assets of the business. It is these assets which earn the profits – part being distributed as an essential counterpart to investment, the balance comprising the retentions mentioned earlier, to complete the loop.

This chart portrays the fundamentals of financial management and it is perhaps salutary to note the incursion of non-accounts on both wings: treasurers on the left (now with their own professional body) and management scientists on the right (shall we see another formal grouping here?)

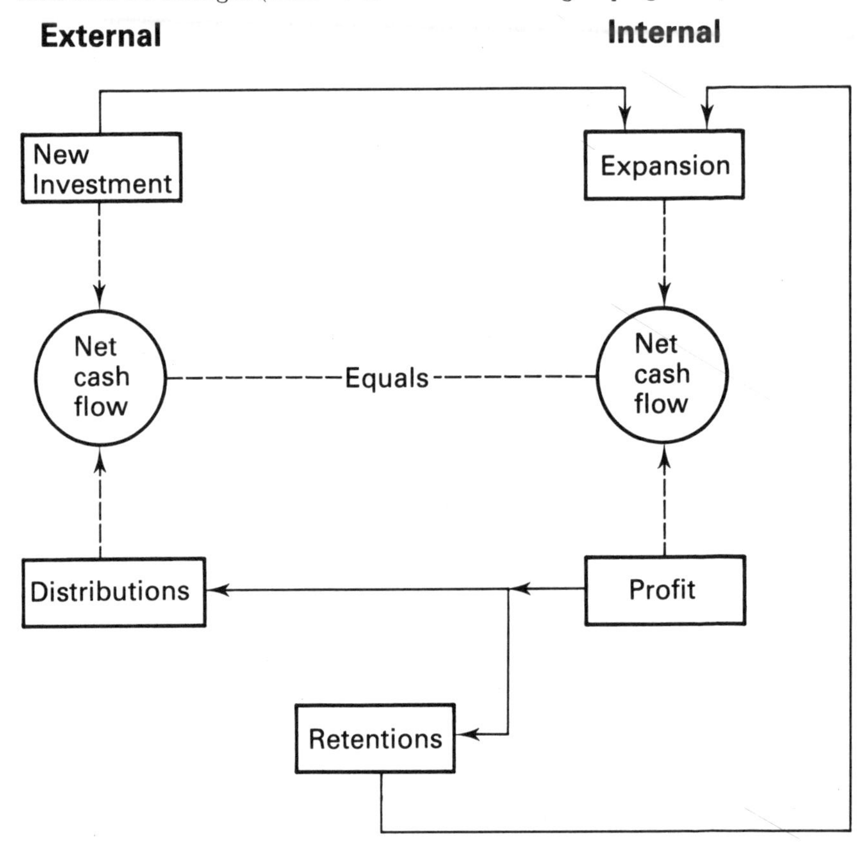

Figure 8.8 The flow of funds

More to the point, however, is the logic of Figure 8.8. Expansion can only be financed by new investment and/or retentions. Given, therefore, that retentions comprise profit minus distributions, we can link the two aspects of cash flow in the equation:

Profit minus Expansion equals Distributions minus Investment

The mark of the top financial manager is that he can discuss cash flow with the controller in terms of profits and expansion, and with the treasurer in terms of distributions and investment – and provide the all-important link between the two in terms of the adequacy of the cash flow under discussion.

He does this by bringing in a further dimension – the most difficult dimension to conceptualise – namely time. What constitutes an adequate cash flow currently is inextricably bound up with its consequences for future cash flows.

On the surface, for example, an increase in cash looks a healthy sign. But if it has been achieved by way of contraction (non-replacement of assets consumed, or even divestment) which substantially reduces the potential for future cash generation, doubts begin to creep in. Conversely, if an absorption or very low generation of cash is caused by expansion (organically or by acquisition) this may be a good thing.

We can go on, as in Figure 8.8, to define profit as cash flow plus expansion (or minus contraction). Simple as it sounds, this is a very powerful definition, for it emphasises the reality. Cash flow is a fact which is precisely ascertainable – internally from the cash book, externally from the published balance sheet. Profit, on the other hand is an interpretation, which is totally dependent on the basis for measuring expansion.

Logically, expansion in this context must mean capacity to generate cash flows, but this is exactly where the time dimension is of the essence. There is no benefit (profit?) in laying out £1 million now in the expectation of receiving a similar amount back in twelve months time. Money costs money, as the treasurer well knows. If the cost of capital (the return necessary to persuade the outside world to invest in the enterprise) is 20% per annum, for example, this provides the criterion for evaluating the worth of such an outlay.

A receipt in excess of £1.2 million in a year's time would suffice to warrant it, as would one in excess of £1.44 million in two years time. £0.2 million a year, increasing at 20% per annum would also suffice; in fact there are an infinite number of possibilities. The approach required is obviously one of discounting future cash flows back to a present value, using the cost of capital of the enterprise as the discount rate.

Such an approach is quite familiar in capital expenditure appraisals. What is far less common is its adaptation to the evaluation of other strategies, to the measurement of the attainment of an adopted strategy, and as an indication of the long-term health of the enterprise and its constituents.

In short, it boils down to defining true expansion as an increase in the net present value of future cash flows discounted at the cost of capital. True profit is then as the result of the expression: Cash flow plus Closing Net Present Value minus Opening Net Present Value, uplifted by the cost of capital.

The introduction, and consistent application of such an approach, guarantees a pivotal role for the management accountant in the strategic management of an enterprise. In short, it provides the framework for strategic financial management.

9 Practical experience of a planner

Raymond Kates

Introduction

Every company has to plan its future in some form and the methods and ideas expressed in the preceding chapters provide an effective framework for the preparation and implementation of short- and long-term plans.

This chapter distills practical experience of the planning function at manager level on matters not already referred to or covered in depth.

The role of the planner

Over the past 12 years I have found that:

1 the same basic principles of planning were applied by three completely different types of company for whom I have worked, viz: Rockware Glass, Alfred Dunhill and Grand Metropolitan,

2 each of these companies then developed a different detailed planning framework based upon their specific organisational structures and products.

3 a common link was the prime concentration upon strategic management, i.e. identifying strategic options open to the company and then translating these into action plans at the business unit level.

A golden rule is that the planning must never be the responsibility of any one management function because planners must always be independent of bias towards any major area of management activity, e.g. finance, production, marketing. The most effective planning is done in those companies in which the planning director or manager is directly responsible to the chairman or chief executive.

The role of the planner is like that of an adviser and it is essential that his personality makes him or her acceptable to other directors and managers. Such a role requires a basic working knowledge of the economic, political, social and market backgrounds within which the company operates so that he is able to assess the likely interaction arising from changes in the environment as well as those originating from management decisions.

A good knowledge of other specialist skills in addition to his own basic qualification enables the planner to work effectively with other personnel who possess a deeper knowledge and experience of such skills. It is a case of knowing enough of the language of other disciplines such as economics, accountancy, marketing and production to communicate effectively with the person concerned.

Effectiveness of the planning function

The effectiveness, and therefore success, of the planning function is dependent upon two key factors:

- **(a)** the complete support of the chief executive (including his acceptance of the modern strategic management concept),
- **(b)** the effectual permeation of planning throughout the whole organisation as a basis for all strategic actions.

Even the best planning systems and personnel in the world will not be successful unless they are fully supported by the chief executive who must be personally responsible for the strategic decision-making process in which planning plays an integral part.

The problems which still exist in many companies attempting to move into strategic management are illustrated in Figure 9.1.

Normal situation	Requirements of strategic management
1 Strategic principles are alien to a chief executive with years of successful operating experience	1 Strategic management has to be the chief executive's top priority
2 Natural forces within the company will draw it towards project thinking and accounting information systems	2 Establishing strategic thinking requires several years of evolution forced by the chief executive
3 The gap between the semantics of strategic planning and accounting planning is enormous	3 Several months of communications sessions with the chief executive are required to get on the same track in respect of: * strategic management concepts * environmental assessment * insights to corporate culture * new investment opportunities

Figure 9.1 Problems of moving into strategic management

One of the chief executive's key roles in planning is to encourage entrepreneurial dynamism within the organisation – a force which can so easily waste away if there is a bureaucratic planning system. Planning must never become an ivory tower activity at head office. It is a vital part of the decision-making process of each individual director and manager. It should involve all levels of employees in the organisation whose work can be directly related to the preparation or achievement of plans. Thus an employee whose work can affect plans should be an active participant in their preparation.

The planning manager should act as a catalyst with all senior managers and place particular emphasis upon the following activities:

- assisting the chief executive to develop coordinated objectives and strategic plans,
- preparing specific business development projects for directors and line managers which relate to future major activities,
- originating ideas and concepts which assist line management in the preparation and presentation of their plans,
- coordinating company or divisional plans and reviewing their relationship to the latest approved objectives and strategies,
- ensuring that approved plans are communicated to all personnel involved in their preparation,
- monitoring progress against agreed action plans to implement strategies and reporting thereon to senior managers.

The planning process must incorporate the following key points if it is to play a major role in strategic decision making:

(a) it should concentrate on the action and keep paperwork to the essential minimum,
(b) it must be a continuous activity (preferably on a roll-over basis) and not a once-a-year special exercise,
(c) it should be judged by the effectiveness of the results achieved and not by the superficial beauty of the planning document.

The first key point above is particularly linked to the KISS (keep it simple, stupid) technique which emphasises the desire of senior managers for simple but effective reports and presentations.

The profit gap

The planning process usually starts with agreement by the Board of the organisation's objectives. Each individual strategic entity (e.g. company or division in a group) then prepares its strategic plan which must be linked to these objectives. Entities which prepare plans at the lowest practicable strategic levels are often called strategic business units (SBUs). Key financial figures are prepared as an appendix to each strategic plan, and are subsequently consolidated and compared with the overall profit objectives. The differences between these consolidated figures and the profit objectives is called the profit gap.

The profit gap is illustrated in Figure 9.2.

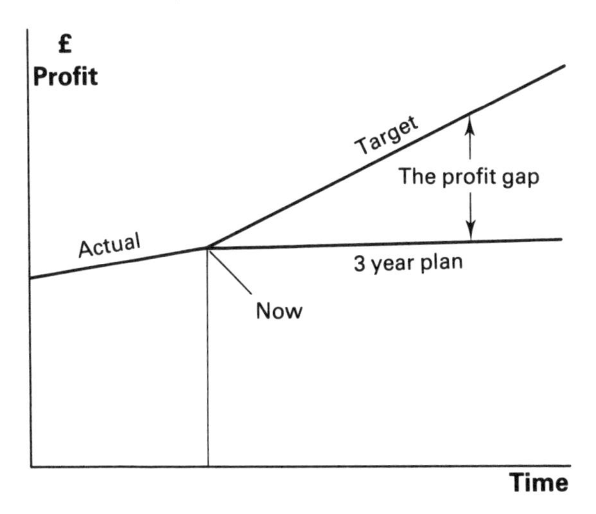

Figure 9.2 The profit gap

The difference between the total of the 3-year plan and the target (overall profit objective) is called the profit gap.

The question is often posed 'Why not set objectives for each company or division so that they equate in total to the above target?' The answer to this is another golden rule of planning – plans must be realistic if they are to succeed. There is no point in setting targets which are not capable of achievement or are excessively easy to attain. Originators of plans should always express what is potentially realistic rather than convey false optimism based on sincere but pious hopes, or, what is equally misleading, false pessimism based on an excessively cautious outlook in the belief that there is real merit in beating an undemanding target!

Ansoff (1968) says that the profit gap:

(a) is the discrepancy between aspirations and anticipations,
(b) can be subdivided into the expansion gap and diversification gap (i.e. between internal and external growth).

Allocation of limited resources

Bearing in mind that profit and cash flow are the objectives in every company, it is worth referring to Bishop's (1977) comments on this subject:

> Many policy problems are related to resource allocation, and the adviser (planner) may be called upon to solve a difficult jig-saw puzzle in proposing how best to fit together limited resources of men, materials, money and machines to best advantage. In all too many cases one could say that the profits are willing but the cash is weak, and the adviser's (planner's) task is then to try and persuade an ambitious entrepreneurial client (company) racing for growth, that they can only succeed by slowing down to allow their cash resources to catch up with their level of trading.

Discussion between directors and managers on the specific financial allocation of limited resources can become verbose, and even ultimately result in a form of Dutch auction if not controlled properly! The linking of resource allocation to approved strategies is of prime importance, and the chief executive of one company managed to obtain complete consensus of his directors by using the format shown in Figure 9.3.

Product	**Product development**	**Distribution companies**		
		Far East	USA	Europe
A	mp	M	M/P	m
B	mp	O	m/P	p
others				

Key

M = Money (promotion and investment)
P = People
The size of the letter indicates whether a high (M/P) or a low (m/p) level of additional money or people will be required.
O = No additional money or people required

Figure 9.3 Allocating limited resources

The method of interpreting the agreed resource allocation for each product can be seen by the following extracts from Figure 9.3.

Product	*Area*	*Allocation of resources*	*Main reason for decision*
A	Product Developed	Low level of additional money and people	Early stage of product life
	USA	High level of additional money and people	Expanding market
B	Far East	No extra resources	Established market
	Europe	No additional money Low level of additional people	Market opportunities achievable by increasing sales force

The subsequent financial plans must reflect the above decisions and equate in total to the limited resources available.

Planning is a continuous process

Planning must be flexible to succeed, and the monitoring and updating of plans to meet changing environmental and market conditions is of prime importance.

The relationship of information to control plays an important part in ensuring a proper feedback process to meet changing circumstances, and is illustrated in Figure 9.4.

The feedback from operational control (middle and junior managers) to tactical planning (senior line managers) monitors current performance against short-term targets. Any anticipated major impact upon medium- and long-term plans is then advised to strategic planning personnel.

Senior management should involve the planning manager in the reviewing and updating of plans resulting from changes to operating conditions and the external environment. In large groups of companies plans are usually monitored on a quarterly basis and include the reconsideration of major strategic issues at SBU, divisional and group levels.

Figure 9.4 also highlights the importance of management information and accounting systems which include such aids and techniques as:

- budgetary control
- key economic indicators
- self-contained projects and programmes
- manpower control
- statistical techniques
- micromodelling packages

Figure 9.4 Relationship of information to control

Strategic decision making

Having referred to some of the key areas of the planning process, I now wish to cover three important questions on strategic decision making:

(a) How does the preparation of strategic plans fit into the planning process timetable in medium and large size companies?
(b) How can major strategic issues be resolved by divisions and translated into action programmes?
(c) What is the next stage of evolution in the key areas of strategic decision making?

The preparation of strategic plans

A simplified example of the planning timetable in a medium or large size group whose financial year ends in March 1986 is shown below:

Stage	*Date*	*Planning Process*	*Prepared by*	*Approval*
1	June 85	GROUP POLICY AND STRATEGIC GUIDELINES	Group Chairman/ Chief Executive	Board
2	Sept 85	DIVISIONAL STRATEGIC OVERVIEW	Divisional CE	Group CE
3	Dec 85	SBU STRATEGIC PLAN + 3 YEAR OUTLINE 1986/7 - 1988/9	SBU CE	Divisional CE
4	Feb 86	SBU 1986/7 BUDGET	SBU CE	Divisional CE

The main objective of the above is to provide a clear strategic direction from the group to the SBUs which will result in rational strategies linked to the resources available.

Major points to note at each stage of the planning timetable are:

STAGE

1 The group policy and strategic guidelines include key strategic issues relating to the group, and cash constraints for each division.

2 The divisional strategic overview translates the group strategic guidelines into its own objectives and then identifies the mission and key strategic tasks (including cash constraints) for each SBU.
3 The SBU strategic plan includes a SWOT analysis (strengths, weaknesses, opportunities and threats) and an action plan for resolving the strategic tasks originated at divisional level.
The 3-year outline incorporates only the key financial and operating figures and concentrates primarily on such matters as the changing environment, competitive position, marketing issues, business development and the profit gap.
4 The 1986/7 budget should represent the detailed interpretation of Year 1 of the 3 year outline approved at stage 3.
Interpretation does not simply mean copying figures from Year 1 of the outline plan. For some SBUs this means adjusting figures to encompass latest conditions even though the strategic assumptions remain unchanged.

It is quite common for a company or division to have a portfolio of separate businesses. Senior managers in this situation have joint responsibility for ensuring that:

1 the motivation, morale and acceptance of profit accountability of the SBU management are maintained by allowing a sufficient level of autonomy,
2 the aggregate financial and operating performance of all the SBUs is in line with the approved company or divisional targets.

The portfolio management techniques usually adopted by companies or divisions to resolve this problem are:

'hands on' for strategy and financial control of major items,

'hands off' for tactics and management style.

So, overall strategy starts at the top and is refined on the way down by the SBU strategy – tactics start at the bottom and get refined on the way up.

The planning process must never slow down the decision-making process in the company, or lead to inflexible strategies, or retard reaction to market changes and opportunities.

Translating strategic issues into action programmes

Returning to the KISS technique, it is important that strategic planning documents are prepared in a clear, concise manner. If they exceed four pages in total, they should be summarised and the objectives to resolve each strategic task should be clearly stated, with each task linked to positive action programmes for its implementation.

The format in Figure 9.5 is an example of how to link the strategic business unit objectives and action plans to divisional strategic tasks. Two objectives have been determined by the SBU management to resolve Divisional Strategic Task 1. The action plan defines how these two objectives will be achieved, as well as by whom and when.

Strategic business unit objectives	Action plan (with milestones)	Person responsible	Completion date on each stage
	Divisional Strategic Task I		
Objective 1	1.1		
	1.2		
Objective 2	1.3		
	1.4		

Figure 9.5 Linking SBU and divisional strategic tasks

In all companies each strategic issue needs to be converted into performable strategic tasks. These in turn should be translated into clear objectives at the SBU level and then followed by action plans to meet each objective.

Figure 9.5 also provides a simple but effective basis for monitoring progress against company or divisional strategic tasks. It is emphasised that all assumptions and objectives must be capable of being monitored in a positive manner, i.e. either quantitatively or qualitatively (e.g. completion by a specified date).

Stages of strategic decision making – company's evolution

Management styles and techniques vary from company to company, and a question continually asked by senior management is "Where are we positioned in the strategic decision-making process compared with other companies?"

In 1981 the Gulf Oil Corporation commissioned a research paper on this subject. It covered 38 major corporations and 14 major consulting firms in the USA, and took twelve months to finalise. Their planning director (Paul, 1982) presented the findings to the 1982 European Corporate Planning conference held in London, and Figure 9.6 clearly illustrates the four major stages of evolution linked to the corporation's value systems, i.e.

- meet budget
- predict future
- think strategically
- create the future

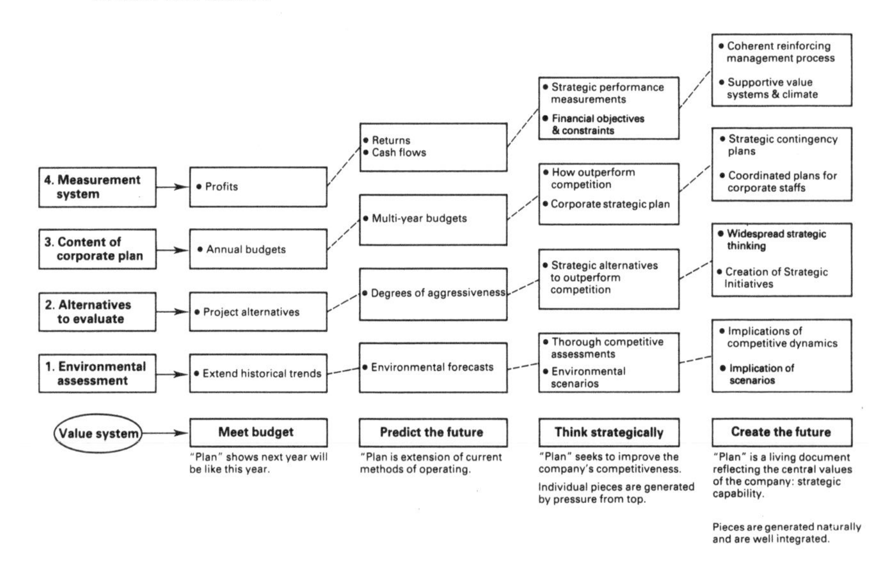

Figure 9.6 Stages of strategic decision making

Most companies are currently positioned between the values 'predict the future' and 'think strategically'. Their degree of development depends upon how far they have progressed in each of the four major elements ranging from environmental assessment to measurement system. Figure 9.6 provides a useful check list for readers to ascertain their own position.

The Gulf Oil Corporation reached four major conclusions from this study:

- many large companies, highly successful for decades now find it difficult to continue their past success,
- continued reliance on centralised accounting-based management will make it difficult for corporate chief executives to chart a successful strategy through an increasingly uncertain future,
- strategically-based management systems are as quantitative as traditional accounting methods but look forward into the external world instead of backward and internally,
- combining the old and the new systems is not a short and easy task – it is long and difficult but can greatly increase the odds of a company's future course being successful.

These conclusions are still very pertinent to many companies within the UK, and were used by Gulf Oil as the rationale behind the implementation of their current strategic decision-making process.

Some of the problems of combining accounting-based and strategy-based systems are referred to in Figure 9.1

Strategies and problems of expansion and diversification

Two of the most important aspects of strategic planning are expansion and diversification. Decisions about them will always play a major part in future company activities, and the following sections briefly cover the key strategic considerations.

The need for expansion and/or diversification arises from the analysis of the profit gap into two distinct parts. The expansion gap relates to increasing the sales of existing products – usually by such means as additional capital investment; acquisition of further technical know-how; entering new markets; or the development and marketing of new products in existing markets. The diversification gap is the part which remains after the strategies and decisions relating to the expansion gap have been determined and usually results in acquisitions in areas already identified in the company's policy and strategic guidelines.

The initial key strategic issue is to determine the amount of cash to be invested in each individual item listed in the analysis of the PROFIT GAP.

The modern acquisition framework is based upon a strategic approach with clearly defined strategic tasks rather than the conventional (financially biased) approach, and the key differences between these are shown in Figure 9.7.

Task	*Strategic approach*	*Conventional approach*
1	Starts with corporate portfolio	Starts with financial projections
2	Identifies strategic criteria for acquisition candidates based upon the company's strategic decision making process	Identifies financial performance criteria for acquisition candidates
3	Concentrates on market valuation – then uses strategic analysis to identify under-valued business potential	Uses financial criteria to screen candidates using historical corporate performance and industry 'fit'
4	Focuses on undervalued strategic assets	Tends to find expensive targets
5	Designed to justify 'premium'	Often fails to justify 'premium'
6	The impact of post-acquisition change is of prime importance	Little or no post acquisition integration

Figure 9.7 The strategic and conventional approach to expansion and diversification

Three key strategic issues relating to whether and how to diversify are:

(a) If existing management's time and expertise is expended on completely new activities will it seriously dilute the performance of existing operations?

(b) Does the culture and background of the company limit the potential areas for diversification, i.e. should there be some direct relationship with existing activities? An example is avoiding diversifying into luxury consumer goods from a base of fast-moving food products.

(c) Does the company have some vicious circle to break? (E.g. what is the risk in moving from UK to international markets?)

Having decided to diversify within specific strategic and cash constraints, the future strategies relating to each possible form of major diversification should be considered. This aspect is illustrated in Figure 9.8.

Type of acquisition	*Future strategies for bidder*
A company with under-utilised financial strength	Use borrowing capacity or other financial strengths (e.g. under-utilised tax loss) to achieve immediate performance premium
An underskilled company in a related industry	Apply superior marketing, technological or production expertise to enhance competitive position and performance
An underexploited physical asset	Anticipate shortages and price increases in the asset's value, and invest to exploit this resource
An undervalued corporate portfolio	Apply more aggresive portfolio management to restructure resource allocation and improve overall results

Figure 9.8 Types of acquisition and related strategies

In my experience, the most important strategic issue is the impact of post-acquisition change. Many of the major problems resulting from diversification are experienced in this area, and examples I have seen include:

- The personalities and skills of managers within the acquired company resulting in early organisational changes contrary to the real longer-term interests and career patterns of the senior managers of the acquiring company.
- Lack of immediate integration and control resulting in a very profitable acquisition becoming a major problem area when key managers retire or leave of their own volition.
- Attempts to force sophisticated management systems upon a small company resulting in the processing of information taking priority over the achievement of its business potential.

All the above items resulted in conflict between the two companies which in turn adversely affected the performance and profit of each. It is therefore stressed that post acquisition strategy must be a key part of acquisition and diversification if such problems are to be avoided.

Current and future developments

Like all management techniques, planning methods and systems have to be flexible and move with the times.

One major development has been the much more extensive use of computerised financial modelling systems to evaluate the 'what if' questions i.e. what impact will various changes in environmental and marketing factors have upon the sales, profit and cash flow of the company?

This development can save many hours of manual evaluation of alternative plans, and can be used by major groups or one-man operations especially with the increasing availability of micro-computer software. Other important technology developments include:

(a) the linking of existing computer programs to public data bases so that environmental and competitive information is immediately available in a format determined by the user,
(b) specialist programs for planners which incorporate key aspects of strategic analysis (e.g. growth share portfolio; investment strategy portfolio),
(c) scenario analysis programs relating to possible future key strategic issues which may affect each individual SBU,
(d) integrated worldwide financial reporting and modelling systems using satellite communications.

More accent is being placed nowadays on competitor analysis. In addition, computer companies are developing 'decision support systems' which they claim will improve the effectiveness of decision making. The latter will ultimately supply personalised menus for each manager covering:

- trend analysis
- competitive comparison
- financial planning
- statistical analysis
- budgeting
- corporate modelling

It is virtually impossible to predict changes in future planning techniques but I have noted particularly that more attention is being given to innovation and the relationship between technological offerings and customer needs.

Technological offerings represent the flexibility of a firm to translate its own technology into specific product designs for different customers, i.e. providing a service in the important areas of design and development which can satisfy a whole range of customer's needs.

Conclusion

It is most important to note the following statement:

> Planning is not an exact science – it helps to identify strategies and key areas of action but its success will always depend upon the effectiveness of management.

In other words: planning is an important aid to, but not a substitute for, effective management.

References and further reading

ADVISORY Council on Applied Research and Development
New opportunities in manufacturing: the management of technology.
London: HMSO, 1983. 96pp.

AGUILAR, F.J. *Scanning the business environment.*
New York: Macmillan, 1967. 239pp

ANSOFF, H. Igor *Corporate strategy.* Harmondsworth:
Penguin, 1970.

ANSOFF, H. Igor *Implanting strategic management.*
Englewood Cliffs, N.J., Prentice Hall, 1984.

BANNOCK, G., BAXTER, R.E., REES, R. *The Penguin Dictionary of Economics.* 2nd ed.
London: Allen Lane, 1979. 467pp.

BECK, P.W. Corporate planning for an uncertain future
Long Range Planning vol. 15 no. 4 Aug. 1982. pp12-21.

BELL, Daniel *The coming of the post-industrial society.* New York:
Basic Books, 1973.

BISHOP, E.B. ACCOUNTING and Auditing in One World, International
Congress of Accountants, 11th, Munich, 10-14 October 1977.
Proceedings . . . Dusseldorf: IdW-Verlag, 1978. 511pp.
'The accountant as management adviser – possibilities and limitations.
General report, E.B. Bishop, pp 317-344.

Boston Consulting Group . . .
Financial Times Management Page 11 Nov. 1981 p14
Ibid. 13 Nov. 1981 p16
Ibid. 20 Nov. 1981 p10

CHANDLER, John and COCKLE, Paul *Techniques of scenario planning.*
Maidenhead: McGraw-hill (UK), 1982. 170pp.

GALBRAITH, Jay R. and NATHANSON, Daniel, A. *Strategy implementation: the role of structure and process.*
St. Paul, Minn.: West Publ. Co., 1978.

HAYES, Robert H. and SCHMENNER, Roger W. How should you organise manufacturing?
Harvard Business Review vol. 56 No. 1 Jan./Feb. 1978. pp105-108.

HEDLEY, Barry Fundamental approach to strategy development.
Long Range Planning vol. 9 No. 6 Dec. 1976 pp 2-11.

HEDLEY, Barry Strategy and the business portfolio.
Long Range Planning vol. 10 No. 1 Feb. 1977. pp 9-15.

HIGGINS, J.C. *Strategic and operational planning systems: principles and practice.*
London: Prentice-Hall International, 1980. 257pp.
Ch. 10 – Social and political forecasting. pp179-191.

HUSSEY, D.E. *Corporate planning: theory and practice.*
Oxford: Pergamon, 1982. 523pp.

HUSSEY, D.E. Strategic management: lessons from success and failure.
Long Range Planning vol. 17 No. 1 Feb. 1984. pp 43-53.

PAUL, A. Dan European Corporate Planning Conference, 4th, London, 1982 "case study", by A. Dan Paul.

PETERS, J.J. and WATERMAN, Robert H. *In search of excellence: lessons from America's best managed companies.*
New York: Harper and Row, 1983.

PORTER, Michael E. *Competitive strategy: techniques for analysing industries and competitors.*
London: Collier Macmillan, 1980. 396pp.

QUINN, J.B. Technology forecasting.
Harvard Business Review vol. 45 No. 2 Mar./Apr. 1967. pp 89-106.

ROBINSON, S.J.Q., WADE, D.P. and HICHENS, R.E. The directional policy matrix – tool for strategic planning.
Long Range Planning vol. 11 No. 3 Jun. 1978. pp 8-15.

ROCKART, J.F. Chief executives define their own data needs.
Harvard Business Review vol 57. No. 2 Mar./Apr. 1979. pp 81-93.

SKINNER, Wickham The focused factory.
Harvard Business Review vol. 52 No. 3 May/Jun. 1974. pp113-121.

SKINNER, W.G. *Manufacturing in the corporate strategy.*
Chichester: J. Wiley, 1978.

SMITH, Adam *The wealth of nations:* edited by Andrew Skinner.
Harmondsworth: Penguin, 1776. (1978 reprint). 535pp.

STEINER, George A. and MINER, John B. *Management policy and strategy: text, readings and cases.*
London: Collier Macmillan, 1977. 1014pp.
in pp189-190.

ZENTNER, René D. Scenarios, past, present and future.
Long Range Planning vol. 15 No. 3 Jun. 1982. pp12-20.

INDEX